POWERFUL PRAYERS FOR YOUR CHILDREN

DAVID AND HEATHER KOPP

WATERBROOK
PRESS

POWERFUL PRAYERS FOR YOUR CHILDREN
PUBLISHED BY WATERBROOK PRESS
2375 Telstar Drive, Suite 160
Colorado Springs, Colorado 80920
A division of Random House, Inc.

ISBN 9781578568505

Printed in the United States of America
2004

146646482

For Neil, Taylor, Noah, Jana, and Nathan

Contents

Foreword

I wonder what deep needs you and your family face today. You may be looking for answers to pressing financial or health concerns. You may have a child or loved one who needs a spiritual awakening. Your marriage may need a fresh wind of understanding, forgiveness, and love. You may want to personally experience more of the nearness of Christ in your daily life.

Friend, your prayers are *meant* to make great things happen. And the very fact that you're holding this book and reading this page tells me that you are about to experience more truth and power, more answers to prayer for yourself and those you love than ever before.

Why would I think that, you wonder?

Because picking up this book indicates something extremely important about you, I believe. It strongly suggests that you are ready to take God at His Word and expect life-changing answers when you pray.

As surprising as it may sound, that desire sets you apart from many believers today. In fact, it's been my observation that millions of contemporary Christians really, honestly *don't* believe that prayer is meant to change things in a big way. They might concede that prayer can help your emotional state or give you more spiritual enlightenment. But prayer that results in observable, even miraculous, answers for us, our families, and our world on a *regular* basis? That kind of belief seems naïve to them, or too self-centered, or just too good to be true.

Interestingly, Jesus Himself made the most astonishing statements in the whole Bible about prayer. For example, He said, "If you abide in Me, and My words abide in you, you will ask what you desire, and it shall be done for you" (John 15:7, NKJV).

As a follower of Jesus, I believe prayer that expects answers is simply faith at work. And faith always begins with taking God at His Word.

Approximately three thousand years ago, one of history's great no-bodies decided to take God at His Word. His name was Jabez. When he looked at himself and his circumstances, he saw no reason to hope, no opportunity for change, and certainly no sign that a miracle might be in store. Yet he prayed a simple, bold prayer that is still changing lives today. You can read his mini-biography and his request in 1 Chronicles 4:9-10. Here is what Jabez prayed, according to the *New King James* translation:

> "Oh that You would bless me indeed, and enlarge my territory, that
> Your hand would be with me, and that You would keep me from
> evil, that I may not cause pain!"

The next sentence records what happened:

> "So God granted him what he requested."

Talk about results! Each of his four requests brought Jabez answers from God, honor in his generation, and an impact among millions who are still learning from his example.

Obviously, how we pray *does* make a difference, and there's much to be learned from Jabez's prayer. But right now I want you to notice one thing in particular: *Jabez desperately wanted to receive what God was waiting to give.*

Let me show you what I mean:

- Jabez cried out for more blessing. God had already promised to bless Abraham and his descendants, and the whole world through them. (See Genesis 12:1-3.)
- Jabez begged for more territory. God had already commanded Moses to conquer and fully occupy all the lands He had given to Israel. (See Deuteronomy 1:8.)

- Jabez pleaded for more of God's power. God had already promised Joshua His presence and power. (See Joshua 1:1-9.)
- And Jabez called out to God for protection from sin and evil. God had already revealed to Israel the choice between "life and good, death and evil" and how to live if they wanted to receive His blessing and protection. (See Deuteronomy 30:15-16.)

It's quite possible that the reason God granted Jabez's requests was that, long after others in Israel had stop expecting very much from God, Jabez still wanted—and asked for—all that God in His goodness had promised!

I've heard from thousands of modern-day Jabezes who are seeing extraordinary results as they pray this scriptural prayer. Not because the words are in any way magical, mind you, but because these individuals are wholeheartedly asking—perhaps for the first time—for God's answers in God's way.

That's where the Powerful Prayers series can help you. Carefully, conscientiously, and expectantly praying Scripture is one way we can know that, as Paul said, we "have the mind of Christ" (1 Corinthians 2:16). Written by my good friends and coworkers David and Heather Kopp, these honest and personal prayers can help you hear God's heart while expressing the deepest desires of your own.

If you're ready to know God better and ask for His very best, this book is for you. I highly recommend it.

May God bless you as you reach for a larger life for His glory and expect greater blessings from Him than you have ever imagined before. Your God is that good, and that ready to answer.

—BRUCE WILKINSON, author, *The Prayer of Jabez*

An Invitation

The prayer book you are holding is composed almost entirely of Scripture, personalized for you as a parent. It is especially for you if you've ever thought, *My prayer life is stuck. If I bore myself, how must God feel?* Or, *My prayers for my children seem weak and ineffective. How can I pray with power and confidence?*

Praying Scripture intentionally can bring a fresh perspective and power to our prayer experience. As a pastor from an earlier time wrote, "Through the Bible God talks to us, and through prayer we talk to God. Few of us are ever prepared to speak to God, until God has spoken to us by His Word."[1] By reflecting attentively on Scripture as we pray, we let the words and desires of Christ dwell richly within us (Col. 3:16). And we understand in a new way the simple petition of Francois Fénelon: "Lord, I know not what I ought to ask of thee; thou only knowest what I need. Teach me to pray. Pray thyself in me. Amen."[2]

As natural and necessary as prayer is to believers, so much of praying remains a God-filled mystery—something *He* does in and through us (Rom. 8:15-16). Is it God's voice or ours, then, that cries over our sleeping children, "Abba Father!"? In these prayers we joyfully answer, "Yes!" It is both!

Our hope is that these written prayers will become your own heartfelt expressions and encourage you to go further in the most important conversation of your life.

DAVID AND HEATHER KOPP

1

The Power of Praying Parents

Those who are wise will shine like the brightness of the heavens, and
those who lead many to righteousness, like the stars for ever and ever.

DANIEL 12:3

The rainy day had ended in a clear, moonless night. "Daddy, everything is washed and ready for bed," Jana, then nine, said wistfully as we walked together in the dark. The air around us was thick with the fragrances of pine and sage. Overhead, the Milky Way gleamed like a river of diamonds between the black trees.

Where the road entered a clearing, we came upon an enormous puddle of rainwater spreading in a thin sheet over the pavement. We paused at its edge, fascinated by the exact reflection of the night sky at our feet. Then, on impulse, we both started walking out into the water.

Or was it into the stars?

"Jana, stand really still," I said when we reached the middle. Barely breathing, we watched between our shoes as the ripples smoothed. Soon the puddle was gone. In its place, first stars, then whole constellations and the stories they tell began to twinkle below us. To the left, Orion the Hunter was about to let fly with his arrow, while to the right the seven sisters of the Pleiades huddled in dainty conversation, oblivious to any threat.

Around us, shadowy pines kept watch as dad and daughter held hands in the dark. Above and below us, the heavens declared another glory.

PART OF SOMETHING GRAND

Becoming a parent is as perspective-changing as wading out into a puddle of stars. Besides the size of the task, there's the mystery of bringing another life into the world. You felt it the first time something fluttered in your womb or your newborn looked up at you as if to ask, "Where did *you* come from?"

From the moment our first child is conceived to the day our last child graduates (and beyond), we know we're part of something grand. We hold our child's hand—feet planted squarely in ordinary life—and point to the kingdom of heaven spreading everywhere around us. "Look!" we urge. "Do you see it now? You live in God's world—it's twinkling all around you. *He* is all around you. And do you realize who you are? You are God's kid!"

Eternity breaks through at every step.

Or at least we hope it will. For all the grandness and wonder, being parents can also be wearing, worrying, and just plain terrifying. For the first time in our lives, so much seems to depend on us—and so much is beyond our power to control. Most of us are never in doubt about our need for God's help.

Maybe that's why being a parent makes praying feel as necessary as breathing.

SO MANY REASONS TO PRAY

If you posted your job priorities as a Christian mom or dad on your fridge, they might look like this:

- raise my kids with love and affirmation
- keep them safe
- teach them the really important things in life
- lead each one into a saving faith in Jesus Christ
- help them become all God intends them to be

Any one of these tasks could make for a lifetime of praying. Taken together, they bring us to our knees, both for our children and for ourselves. The theologian Karl Barth once said, "To clasp the hands in prayer is the beginning of an uprising against the disorder of the world."[1] Any mom with a two-year-old understands him perfectly.

Prayer is a God-given part of our urge to protect, care for, and shape the offspring He has given us. Yet we don't pray just to accomplish our parental goals; we pray to grow in wisdom ourselves, to recover, to hold on. And we pray to give thanks. "Children are a gift from God; they are his reward" (Ps. 127:3, TLB). As a couple blessed with the gift of children, we've seen that raising kids is biologically, emotionally, and spiritually at the center of what our lives are to be about. That's something to celebrate.

Often we pray simply because we have to talk. We *long* to talk to the Person who holds together everything we hold dear and who is Himself most dear to us. And ultimately this is why we pray: because knowing God and His love is our greatest treasure. We see it shining like a million stars all around. Life is hard, but our treasure is true, and we want to pass it on to our children. Jesus said that anyone who found this treasure in a field would sell everything he owned to possess it. David called it "the heritage of those who fear your name" (Ps. 61:5).

Among readers of *Christian Parenting Today* magazine, the greatest single concern about raising children is that the treasure will somehow get lost. One Wisconsin mom wrote, "I trust in the Lord and His promises, yet my biggest worry is having one of my daughters turn away from the Lord." Another said, "So many good parents are finding their children are abandoning their faith as they get older. Right off the top of my head, I can think of nine families who live with the heartache of a child or two or even three who have rejected God."[2]

Our concerns can make us so focused on getting God's help with our parenting tasks that we may overlook the fact that He has also asked for our help. He has invited us to make a difference—in fact, to ask for miracles in Jesus' name. Like the Levites of old, we parents are invited to fulfill a priestly role in our families.

STANDING IN THE GAP

Consider the priests of Old Testament times who helped bridge the gap between God and man. While serving in the temple courts, they pronounced blessings, taught God's Word, led in confession and worship, presented offerings and sacrifices on behalf of the faithful, and made sure the lamps (signifying God's presence) were always lit. Like them, we parents stand in the gap for those over whom God has given us charge.

We stand before God to plead on behalf of our kids. "Lord, help Nathan do well on his test today. Show him that You care about every detail of his life." In this role we are intercessors; we pray on behalf of someone else. The priest Samuel understood the gravity of his role as spiritual father for the children of Israel when he promised the people,

"Far be it from me that I should sin against the LORD by failing to pray for you" (1 Sam. 12:23).

Interceding for our kids is obviously important, but a wonderful truth about prayer is that *as we pray* we receive greater strength and insight to "stand before our kids" as well, to plead on behalf of our God. "Nathan, the Lord knows what you're up against today. He'll be with you. He's promised." In this role we are teachers, leaders, encouragers. Moses exhorted the Jews to teach God's laws to their children at every opportunity, "talking about them when you sit at home and when you walk along the road, when you lie down and when you get up" (Deut. 11:19).

Jesus' prayer for His disciples, recorded in John 17, beautifully illustrates how these roles of intercessor and ambassador come together. Jesus stood in the gap for His disciples. On the one hand, He made an appeal for their future—for their safety, unity, and spiritual growth. On the other, He told the Father that He had obediently delivered God's appeal to His followers. In so many ways Jesus' prayer expresses the mission of a Christian parent: "[Father,] I have revealed you to those whom you gave me out of the world. They were yours; you gave them to me. . . . Now they know that everything you have given me comes from you. For I gave them the words you gave me and they accepted them" (John 17:6-8).

THE POWER OF A PARENT'S PRAYER

God doesn't ask us to pray just to put us through the motions. We're invited to be advocates with authority and power. The Bible offers many examples of parents who demonstrated a conviction that their prayers could effect great change. Samson's parents asked God to send an angel to teach them how to raise the boy who had been promised to them. Job regularly offered prayers and sacrifices for his seven sons and three daughters. Abraham pleaded with God to bless his outcast son, Ishmael.

God's love incarnated in praying people always changes lives (James 5:16). And as parents we are in first position to make great use of that power to claim our children for God. Because we know them best and care the most, we can pray fervently and with genuine insight. Other influences—good and bad—may prevail in our children's lives for a while, but they never come first or last longest. A mother is, as someone has said, the first book read and the last put aside in every child's library.

The apostle Paul reminded young Timothy of the sincere faith that had been handed down through his family—from his grandmother Lois to his mother, Eunice, to Timothy himself. As Timothy's spiritual father, Paul knew that he too had power in the young man's life. Paul told his "dear son," Timothy, that he was in his prayers night and day. "Continue in what you have learned and have become convinced of, because you know those from whom you learned it, and how from infancy you have known the holy Scriptures" (2 Tim. 1:3,5,14; 3:14-15). Timothy seemed to struggle with timidity and self-doubt. Yet the power of praying parents was at work. Timothy went on to serve as a faithful bishop and even to die a martyr for his Lord.

FREEDOMS IN THE FAMILY

Praying is the sound God's family makes when we are in right relationship with our Lord. The spectrum of that sound includes praise, thanksgiving, confession, petition, intercession, worship—the wonderful hubbub of earnest talking and listening between children and a heavenly Father.

We have tremendous freedom in our praying:

- We can pray anywhere, anytime (Jon. 2:1; 2 Tim. 1:3).
- We can wail out our deepest, most troubling feelings and know God will not be shocked or deaf to our pleas (Ps. 102:17; Lam. 2:19).
- We can pray haltingly, simply, confusedly (Rom. 8:26; Ps. 69:33).
- We can pray alone or with other believers (Dan. 6:10; Acts 2:42-47).
- We can pray ecstatically, carried along by God's Spirit, or woodenly, driven by our commitments when all feelings fail us (Eph. 5:18-19; Ps. 102:23-28).
- We can pray silently, wordlessly (Ps. 5:1; Matt. 6:6).
- We can pray over and over for the same thing (Luke 18:1-8).

And *Praying the Bible for Your Children* celebrates yet another rewarding freedom in our praying: We can speak Scripture back to God, making it the sincere expression of our own hearts (Col. 3:16). We'll explain this thoroughly in the next chapter.

HOW TO PRAY EFFECTIVELY

While God has given us freedom in prayer, He has also given us help. In the Word we find specific instructions for how to pray effectively. With the Holy Spirit's aid, we can make them part of a successful prayer experience.

Pray reverently. Keep in mind God's holiness and greatness. Pray with genuine respect and humility (Eccles. 5:1-2; Matt. 6:9).

Pray sincerely. The words don't matter as much as your heart. Bring a deeply felt desire to see God act for your children and a wholehearted willingness to do your part to make God's solutions possible (Matt. 6:7-8; Heb. 10:22; Ps. 51:17).

Pray in faith. Simply and completely trust in God's commitment to your family's best interests and in His power to act on your behalf (Jer. 32:17; Heb. 11:6).

Pray with purity. Don't let your prayers be hindered by known sin in your heart or life: unfinished business with God, your neighbor, or your own family members (Prov. 15:8; Mark 12:38-40; 1 John 3:21-22; James 4:8).

Pray according to God's will. Submit your personal desires to God's greater glory and purposes. Test your wishes for your kids against His revealed truth (1 John 5:14; Matt. 6:10).

Pray in Jesus' name. We have access to the Father only through Jesus' name and by His merits. His name is the power above all powers on earth (John 15:16; Eph. 2:18).

Pray thankfully. Recalling God's past goodness and His faithful character, surround every new request with thanksgiving and praise (Phil. 4:6; Ps. 22:3).

Pray boldly and persistently. Jesus taught that a loving Father is waiting to give us His best, and it's better than we could ever imagine. Make your requests known, and continue to expect answers (Heb. 4:16; Luke 18:1-8; Acts 12:5).

A GOD WHO ANSWERS

Praying effectively doesn't mean that we always get what we want.
Scholars cite 650 prayers in the Bible (outside the book of Psalms,
which forms a prayer book of its own), and 450 of these prayers have
recorded answers. What, we wonder, makes some prayers "work" while
others don't appear to?

At times we must go forward in faith when God's answers to deeply
felt concerns remain wrapped in mystery. When her baby died after a
grueling series of medical interventions, one Texas mother still believed
God had responded to her prayers. "God heard my prayers," she said.
"He knew my desires and expectations and answered in this way for
reasons only He understands."

Jesus promised that every prayer of a God-seeking person would be
answered. "Everyone who asks receives," He said (Matt. 7:8). Always.
The answer—which may at first appear to be no answer—may be yes
or no, direct or indirect, immediate or deferred. Sometimes the change
we initially seek outside of ourselves ("Please make Natalie stop whining") becomes a prayer for change within ("Lord, teach me how to slow
down and listen to my daughter").

How good it is to know that when we parents pray we can be certain our petitions are always received and responded to by a loving
Father. "Which of you, if his son asks for bread, will give him a stone?"
Jesus asked. "If you, then, though you are evil, know how to give good
gifts to your children, how much more will your Father in heaven give
good gifts to those who ask him!" (Matt. 7:9,11).

An Amazing Opportunity

When we accept God's invitation to a praying ministry in our families, we are often surprised to discover how much our own lives change. Not only do we gain a very real advantage over the forces that war against our children each day, but we also benefit personally. Repeatedly and gently we're reminded of God's parent-heart for us. We receive the peace and joy He has promised. And we discover new insights into old problems.

On this journey of prayer we never pray alone. We are actually joining with Christ in His greatest work in heaven today. He too stands before the Father interceding for His children—us!—as well as our children (Rom. 8:34). And He gives us His Spirit to help us as we pray (Rom. 8:26-27).

When you think about it, the opportunity to pray is an amazing invitation from the one who loves us most. Almost as hard to resist as a puddle full of stars. As you pray the prayers within this book, may you feel Him take your hand and lead you gently into the center of what may look like ordinary family stresses and messes—and find eternity waiting for you.

CHAPTER 2

Why Pray the Bible?

My heart trembles at your word.
I rejoice in your promise
  like one who finds great spoil.

PSALM 119:161-162

Prayer—conversation with God—is simple enough to be understood and experienced by a five-year-old. The day our son Taylor asked Jesus to come into his heart, he and Mom were parked in front of Dairy Queen slurping milkshakes. But the moment was right. As traffic rolled by and ice cream melted, a child and his God talked. A life changed forever. So simple.

So why is it that even when we're praying for the ones we love most, we find ourselves wondering if we really know how to pray? We often become tongue-tied, repetitious, dull. Our prayers can dwindle to worries we breathe half-aloud through the day or to routines we deliver half-aware before meals and at bedtime. *Surely there's more to prayer than this*, we hope. Deep down, we want to pray in a way that makes a difference in us, those we love, and our world. We want to deeply enjoy God's presence, receive His blessings, and be changed into His glorious likeness. We want a prayer life that works.

When we turn to the Bible itself, we find the help we're looking for.

GOD'S PRAYER BOOK

The Bible is a ready-made prayer book for God's family. We "pray the Bible" when we use passages of Scripture to form prayers or when we say the verses directly back to God, making them our own petitions. Whenever we speak to God with the words of God, we move closer to the kind of vital, effective prayer life we long for.

Several years ago I (David) realized I'd been praying the Bible all my life—I'd just never called it that before. My first experiences came through my missionary parents. In spite of a serious speech impediment, my father, Joe Kopp, preached the Word at every opportunity. He used Scripture memorization both to help him overcome his stammer and to teach illiterate Africans the Bible. Saying Bible passages back to God became part of every village church service as well as many of our meal and bedtime prayers.

Heather and I have continued to make Scripture prayers a part of our family experience. The opportunities are so varied:

- the life verse my mother has faithfully prayed for me, now prayed by Heather and me for one of our sons: "I'm confident of this, that He who began a good work in you will carry it on to completion" (from Phil. 1:6);

- a screen-saver blessing on the family computer, which reminds us each to bring all our cares to God: "The LORD will fulfill His purpose for you. His love for you endures forever—and He never abandons the works of His hands!" (from Ps. 138:8);

- praises from Scripture written in colored chalk on the foundation of our new house, like: "The Lord is good, a refuge in times of trouble. He cares for those who trust in him" (Nah. 1:7).

Praying the Bible is not new theology. Neither is it some kind of magical mumbo jumbo. Yet it is a source of power. Jesus often used Scripture in His prayers for Himself and His disciples. Throughout the Bible, we see examples of godly men and women incorporating God's promises and commands in their petitions to Him. They used the Word in their prayers for encouragement, calling to mind who God is and what He has done. Jesus and His disciples sang the psalms together as part of morning and evening prayers. And at the moment of His greatest agony on the cross, Jesus cried out the words of a psalm: "My God, my God, why have you forsaken me?" (Ps. 22:1).

Many other Bible passages are recorded prayers. Some of the best known are the prayer of Moses after the escape through the Red Sea (Exodus 15); Hannah's song at the temple (1 Samuel 2); Jeremiah's lament over Jerusalem (Lamentations); Jonah's plea for grace (Jonah 2); the song of Mary after the angel's visit (Luke 1:46-55); "The Lord's Prayer" (Matt. 6:9-13); Jesus' prayer for His disciples (John 17:6-19); and Paul's prayers for a young church (Eph. 3:14-21, 6).

Since the time of Christ, Christians throughout the world have used the book of Psalms as an unofficial prayer book for the church, and prayer books designated for public worship contain some of our most enduring examples of Scripture-based prayers. For example, "The Great Thanksgiving," from *The Book of Common Prayer*, is taken from Romans 12:1: "And here we offer and present unto thee, O Lord, ourselves, our souls and bodies, to be a reasonable, holy, and living sacrifice unto thee."[1] Since the Jesus Movement of the 1970s, singing choruses of Scripture back to God has become a vibrant part of church worship in many circles.

Praying the Bible for Your Children applies this principle to personal prayer. C. S. Lewis, among many others, used written, Bible-based prayers in his devotional life. Lewis said this helped him concentrate, stay doctrinally sound, and know how to pray. Otherwise, he said, "the crisis of the present moment, like the nearest telegraph post, will always loom largest."[2]

When we pray with the Bible as our guide, we hear God's voice more clearly, and we find creative ways to let God's teachings live in and through us.

Consider some of the benefits of praying Scripture:

Praying the Bible gets us "unstuck." Sometimes we're not diligent in prayer because we have a record of mediocre experiences with it—we get distracted, bored, vague. Mostly we have a hard time getting started. Words and ideas fail us. Praying intentionally with Scripture in mind is like choosing to follow a map in new territory. Suddenly we can spot several worthy destinations. We can pray confidently and specifically: "Help Neil to understand that if he'll just acknowledge you as Lord today, you will show him how to solve this problem" (Prov. 3:6).

Praying the Bible helps us get our memory back. Sometimes we feel so overwhelmed by feelings and needs that our prayers don't seem to reach beyond the problem. We forget God's character, promises, past faithfulness, goodness, and even His extravagances with us. Praying the truths of the Bible helps us remember what God has done and what He can still do.

Jeremiah was an emotional priest called to speak for God during the siege and fall of Jerusalem. When he focused on the terrors around him, Jeremiah felt personally assaulted, even abandoned by God: "He pierced my heart with arrows from his quiver" (Lam. 3:13). Only when he focused on God's past mercies did he find strength and encouragement: "Yet this I call to mind and therefore I have hope: Because of the LORD's great love we are not consumed, for his compassions never fail" (3:21-22).

Praying the Bible helps us pray more specifically and in line with God's will. Without intending to, we can pray ignorantly, even at cross-purposes with what God wants. Jesus told the Pharisees, "You are in error because you do not know the Scriptures or the power of God" (Matt. 22:29). In the same way we use the Bible to measure the content of a sermon or lesson, we can use Scripture to test our motives and reveal the big picture. When we pray the Bible back to God, we speak to God in the words of God with the truth of God. This encourages us to go beyond "Lord, keep Noah safe today" to a more complete expression: "Lord, You've promised to contend fiercely with every circumstance and power for Noah's life (Isa. 49:25-26). You have commanded Your angels to guard him (Ps. 91:11). Be Noah's champion today, as You've promised (Isa. 43:5-7). Thank You, heavenly Father!" In this kind of prayer we bring God's revealed will into our thoughts, not just our problem or our wishes for a resolution. And when we pray in line with God's will, He promises to answer (1 John 5:14).

Praying the Bible helps us pray with confidence and expectancy. When we know and use Bible truths, we can pray with a more muscular faith. Wayne Spear points out that some Bible promises make God's response so definite that the only sensible expectation on our part is complete confidence. For example, when we pray for the forgiveness of sin, God is committed to one, unfailing response. It's spelled out in 1 John 1:9: "If we confess our sins, he is faithful and just and will forgive us our sins and purify us from all unrighteousness."[3]

Faith is not a belief that "anything can happen," writes Spear, but a confidence that *what God has promised will happen.*[4] When we pray in harmony with the principles of Scripture, we can be sure that our needs will be met even though we leave the how and when to God.

Praying the Bible helps us nurture a growing relationship with God. Prayer is an ongoing conversation between two very interested parties, and the Bible is the major part of God's end of the conversation. Imagine a young couple who becomes engaged only to be suddenly separated for months by the husband's military service. Every day the man sends his fiancée a lengthy letter, telling her about his daily activities, describing his hopes and dreams for their future, talking about his likes and dislikes. But when the couple finally reunites, his beautiful bride-to-be is completely in the dark about his life, his promises, and plans. Before long they lapse into silence. One day the young woman complains that her suitor never tells her what he's really thinking. "I'm not really sure you care about me!" she finally exclaims. After some painful probing the truth comes out: The woman has never actually read her mail. "Usually I just opened the letters to see if you still loved me," she admits. "And, well, I saved them all carefully . . ."

When we fail to bring Scripture into our prayer conversation, we can be as confused about who God is as this woman was about her husband-to-be. We struggle needlessly with doubts about God's intentions toward us and our children simply because we haven't read, believed, or remembered His love letter to us.

Praying the Bible can open our hearts to allow the Spirit to minister to us. Scripture leads us into an encounter with the Father-heart of God. We hear our Father's voice: "Fear not, for I have redeemed you; I have summoned you by name; you are mine" (Isa. 43:1). And we bask in His presence. This is the attitude David described in Psalm 131: "I have stilled and quieted my soul; like a weaned child with its mother." Scriptures like this remind us that we are invited to come to God with nothing to give, only with who we are—listening, surrendering, perhaps broken and in need of comfort or healing. Henri Nouwen said this act, which he called "praying with open hands," requires the greatest courage of all.[5]

WHAT PRAYING THE BIBLE DOESN'T MEAN

Praying the Bible doesn't mean we have to leave out our untidy humanness when we talk with God. The Bible leads us toward the truth about our humanity, not away from it. Consider how many of David's psalms begin with a cry from the depths of his very human soul. Paul repeatedly asked God to free him from his "thorn in his flesh." Even Jesus begged God to "take this cup from me." God longs for honest communication with us. Unlike the cashier at the grocery store, when God asks, "How are you today?" He really wants to know. Of course we can't hide our real thoughts and feelings from God anyway. But because we approach God through Christ's righteousness, we can be sure that God receives us with grace, regardless of our human condition (Heb. 10:19-22).

Praying the Bible doesn't mean we pray with magical powers. We pray "magically" when we believe that a certain arrangement of words, like the right coins inserted in a vending machine, will guarantee the same result every time. It's true that the Bible tells us we have access to power in Jesus' name, that there is power in the Word, and that God promises to release His power through our faith. But we don't ever leverage God or control His will, no matter how we pray. Our fallen world comes complete with chaos, tragedy, uncertainty, randomness, and personal trials of all kinds. Jesus' promise to us is not that we can magically escape them through prayer but that we can overcome them.

Praying the Bible is not about using fancy language or sounding "religious." In Matthew 6, Jesus warned about praying aloud just to look more "spiritual" to others and about bombarding God with excess words in hopes that He will hear us better. We don't need to "talk better" to be acceptable to God, nor can we manipulate or impress Him with our carefully worded prayers.

The true test of our praying lies in our simple faith and a pure devotion to God's will. These prayers, for example, are both elegant and complete:

- A mother whispers, "Lord, protect my baby!" as she leans over the crib in early morning darkness.
- A father with a struggling teen clings to Christ's promise: "No one can snatch them out of my hand" (John 10:28).
- A little boy outside a Dairy Queen with ice cream on his shirt squeezes his eyes shut and starts to pray, "Jethuth, pleathe come in . . ."

And God delights to hear.

MAKING THESE PRAYERS YOUR OWN

In the pages that follow, you'll find Scripture-based prayers in a variety of formats. References in the text point the way to the Bible passage at hand. The words of the Bible are used as they appear in Scripture or modified slightly for personal application, or the prayer addresses a given passage or collection of verses. Some of the meditations are brief enough to memorize easily or to copy onto paper and slip into a handbag or school notebook.

In an effort to represent the range of concerns all of us parents share, Heather and I identified nine categories: a parent's preparation; protection and deliverance; worship and affirmation; family and friends;

learning and giving; spiritual growth; character development; specific son and daughter concerns; and the future.

We encourage you to keep *Praying the Bible for Your Children* on your nightstand or in your briefcase and use it as part of your daily devotional time.

You can also use the index to help you track down a prayer either by title or by topic. We've kept the topical index simple; subjects are arranged under eight felt-need categories like, "Lord, as a parent I feel . . ." and "Lord, help my child to learn . . ."

While prayer can seem costly to us when we're tired, as moms and dads we easily understand Paul when he says to his "children" in Corinth: "I am jealous for you with a godly jealousy. . . . I will very gladly spend for you everything I have and expend myself as well" (2 Cor. 11:2; 12:15).

As you spend yourself in prayer on behalf of your precious children, we pray that the Holy Spirit will use this book to encourage you—and that you'll quickly "pass beyond reading into praying."[6]

In Jesus' name we pray—and are confident—that the God who gives endurance, encouragement, and hope (Rom. 15:5,13) will accomplish immeasurably more than all you can ask or imagine because His own power—the same power that raised Jesus from the dead (1 Pet. 1:21)—is at work in you and in the children you love (Eph. 3:20).

DAILY
PRAYERS

"Speak, Lord—I'm Listening . . ."

Then Eli realized that the LORD was calling the boy. So Eli told Samuel, "Go and lie down, and if he calls you, say, 'Speak, LORD, for your servant is listening.'" So Samuel went and lay down in his place.

The LORD came and stood there, calling as at the other times, "Samuel! Samuel!"

Then Samuel said, "Speak, for your servant is listening."

I SAMUEL 3:8-10

O Lord God,
Please call my children to You by name as You called Samuel and as You have called me (Isa. 43:1). Thank You that You promise to knock patiently on the door of each heart in this family (Rev. 3:20). Thank You that You pursue us (Ps. 139:5)! You did it for me—do the same for each of my children.

Yes, pursue them, Lord. Keep calling them—as You did with Samuel—until each child has said, "Yes, Lord. I'm listening."

Your promise of salvation is for children of all ages—in fact, for everyone who answers Your call (Acts 2:39; Rom. 10:13). Thank You for Your promise that as my children hear You and believe in You, they will pass from death to life (John 5:24)!

May I be like Eli, who encouraged Samuel to say yes to You. May I never hinder my children from responding to You (Mark 10:14). May I never say, "Not now, honey." Or, "You're too young."

And far beyond the first "Yes, Lord!" may my children listen carefully to Your voice and answer quickly as long as they live.

In Jesus' name. Amen.

Blankies and Binkies

When I became a man my thoughts grew far beyond those of my childhood, and now I have put away the childish things.

1 CORINTHIANS 13:11, TLB

Dear Lord Jesus,

When You lived on earth, You set a maniac free from his demons. You set a smart lawyer free from his ignorance. You set Lazarus free from the grave and a world free from sin.

Can You help with baby pacifiers? Or with the T-rex who lives in our basement? I'm coming to You humbly today for help with those annoying habits and unreasonable obsessions that my children cling to. These little fixations now—whether it's ratty blankies, nail-biting, or video games—remind me of the frightening addictions that can come later.

Lord, where Your spirit is, there is freedom (2 Cor. 3:17). Dwell in my children in great power. Thank You that You are always at work in my kids, if they invite You, to give them both the will and the ability to live as You want (Phil. 2:13).

Teach me to be a liberator for my children, like Moses was for the children of Israel (Exodus 1–20). I want to lead them away from any slavery even if, at the time, they love it. Help us as a family to become experts at "free living"—to nip unwise behaviors in the bud. And yet give us the common sense to accept normal attachments as passing things, to encourage one another constantly, and to wrap each other in a secure and unconditional love that casts out all fears (1 John 4:18).

In Your name. Amen.

Sweeter Than Honey

How sweet are your words to my taste.

PSALM 119:103

PRAYING FROM PSALM 19

Lord,
Today I pray that my children would love Your Word.

Because "the law of the LORD is perfect, reviving the soul," may my children realize how much they need Your refreshment (v. 7).

Because "the statutes of the LORD are trustworthy," may my children take risks to build their lives on Your Word (v. 7).

Because "the precepts of the LORD are right, giving joy to the heart," may my children take genuine delight in studying the Bible (v. 8).

Because "the commands of the LORD are radiant, giving light to the eyes," may my kids use Your Word to make important decisions (v. 8).

Because "the fear of the LORD is pure, enduring forever," may my children revere, honor, and worship You all of their lives (v. 9).

Because "the ordinances of the LORD are sure and altogether righteous," may my children rely on them to test every other belief, philosophy, or lifestyle they encounter (v. 9).

Because your ordinances "are sweeter than honey," may my children crave the Bible more than any other book (v. 10).

I pray, Lord, that by loving Your Word, my children will receive important warnings about life and be blessed with great personal reward (v. 11).

Amen.

Parents Are Priests

You . . . are being built into a spiritual house to be a holy priesthood,
offering spiritual sacrifices acceptable to God through Jesus Christ.

1 PETER 2:5

Heavenly Father,

In ways I hardly understand You have called me to have a priestly role
in my own household. How desperately I need to be clothed in Your
righteousness as I lead and teach my children to respond to You
(Ps. 132:9). Help me learn from our merciful and faithful great high
priest, Jesus:

He understands and has compassion on our weaknesses (Heb.
4:15)—Lord, give me empathy when my child is crabby, tired, or selfish.

Jesus is our daily champion and advocate before the Father's high
throne (Heb. 2:17; 4:14)—Lord, show me how to intercede faithfully
and fervently for my children. You have called me to be a prayer champion for each one of them.

Jesus is our mediator and bridge to life (1 Tim. 2:5, John 14:6)—
Lord, make me an effective go-between as I try to communicate Your
truths to my children and lead them to You.

Finally, Father, help me to pray faithfully for my kids, being a good
example of the importance of confession and worship. May I be a witness morning and night of Your love and faithfulness (Ps. 92:2).

How thankful I am for Your Son, Jesus Christ, who loves me and
has freed me from my sins by His blood and has made me a priest to
serve You (Rev. 1:5-6).

Amen.

Giving a Priestly Blessing

Part of our priestly role as parents is to pronounce blessings on our kids. We do this whenever we say something like, "The Lord has His hand on you, Tommy!"

Moms and dads can also repeat blessings from the Bible to their children. The following blessing was given by Aaron and his son to the Israelites:

"The LORD bless you and keep you;

the LORD make his face shine upon you

and be gracious to you;

the LORD turn his face toward you

and give you peace."

NUMBERS 6:24-26

Gifted Kids

Each one should use whatever gift he has received to serve others.

1 PETER 4:10

Lord,

Thank You that You made each of my children unique, with different passions and talents. Truly, You are the giver of every good gift (James 1:17). Thank You for opportunities my children have to express their interests and abilities, from basketball to ballet, from team roping to tie-dyeing.

Thank You also for the spiritual gifts You are nurturing in them to build up the fellowship of other believers—gifts like teaching, service, comforting others, and healing (1 Cor. 12:8-10).

Today I pray that my kids would want and value the treasures You have invested in them for their own benefit and for the blessing of others (1 Cor. 14:1-5). And beyond that, plant in them a lifelong desire to use any talent—be it physical, mental, or spiritual—to serve You (1 Cor. 12:4-11).

Help me to be the kind of encourager my children need in order to persist in their areas of talent. May I be like Paul, who urged Timothy, "Do not neglect your gift, which was given you" (1 Tim. 4:14). And help my kids work hard to make the most of the gifts You've given them—to practice, learn, and train with patience and diligence.

Thank You for Your promise, Lord, that whatever good work You begin in my child, You will continue to bring to fullness as he or she seeks You (Phil. 1:6).

Amen.

So Many Wonders

Sons are a heritage from the LORD, children a reward from him.

PSALM 127:3

My Heavenly Father,
On behalf of my family today, I bring You offerings of thanks for what You have done. You have opened Your hands and rewarded us with children, gifts from heaven.

Lord, You have breathed Your breath of life into our family. You have knit together babies in the womb (Ps. 139:13). You have surrounded the lonely with children (Ps. 113:9). You have given us honor and fulfillment as parents (Prov. 17:6). O God, Your works on our behalf are wonderful (Ps. 139:14)!

Now, as I name my children in Your presence, I pause to offer specific thanks for each child . . .

Father, I know that sometimes Your blessings are disguised as a challenge or a disappointment. As I listen for Your voice about my children, show me what I may have overlooked or undervalued.

All day, help me see past the responsibilities and routines, the hassles and worries, and remember to celebrate. When I look across the table at mealtime, may I see more than bad manners and hear more than demands. May I see You in their eyes and hear Your voice, for "of such is the kingdom of God" (Luke 18:16, KJV).

Many, O Lord, are the wonders You have done at our house—more than I had even thought (Ps. 40:5)!

Thank You in Jesus' name. Amen.

The Way of Angels

See that you do not look down on one of these little ones. For I tell you
that their angels in heaven always see the face of my Father in heaven.

MATTHEW 18:10

Dear Lord,
Sometimes I wake in the night with a jolt. I feel how helpless I am, ultimately, to make life turn out okay for my little ones, to keep accidents,
evil, and disease from touching them.

My angels encamp around those who fear Me, and deliver them (from
Ps. 34:7).

Thank You, Lord. When I'm afraid for my children, my first impulse is to run to You. All our hopes are in Your hands.

If you make Me your refuge, then no disaster will overwhelm you. I
will command My angels to guard you and your children in all your ways
(from Ps. 91:9-11).

Help me to remember that Your spiritual warriors can shut the
mouths of lions and defeat the agents of Satan (Ps. 103:20, Dan. 6:22).
Thank You for Your angels of mercy and power who guard even the
weakest in Your kingdom.

My angels are ministering spirits sent to serve those who will inherit my
salvation (from Heb. 1:14).

Lord, I choose to accept the risks of living, knowing that my children are held in Your strong embrace for all eternity.

Amen.

Here Among Us

What other nation is so great as to have their gods near them the way the LORD our God is near us whenever we pray to him?

DEUTERONOMY 4:7

Lord,

I rest in Your presence today. I put aside all my endless worries. I do not pick up any requests, except this one: *Make Your presence known to my children.*

We are Your family, and You live always in the company of Your people (Ps. 14:5). You inhabit my children's simplest prayers and off-key praises (Ps. 8:2). You never leave them for a second (Heb. 13:5). You are their Lord. Unstuff their ears, open their eyes, melt their hearts with Your compelling reality. Show them how much they need Your "here-ness" today.

Be here! Be here! In the clanging kitchen, out in the yard or street, in the silent room where a toddler sleeps, in hallways, in the daydreams of teenagers, in the to-do lists of Mom and Dad, in every hour of our day . . . be here among us, O God! Help me hear You say, "I am always with you. It is good to be near me" (from Ps. 73:23,28).

You, Great God, are our life. Let Your Spirit sing in my children's innermost beings today. And let our spirits sing in You and bring You joy. All day long.

Amen.

Busy Waiting

I say to myself, "The LORD is my portion; therefore I will wait for him."
The Lord is good to those whose hope is in him, to the one who seeks
him; it is good to wait quietly for the salvation of the LORD.

LAMENTATIONS 3:24-26

Dear Lord,

My son sees his name in lights up ahead—and he wants it now. He's
counting on stardom by Christmas but hasn't had his first gig yet. And
my daughter wants to dance like Nureyev, but she's still having trouble
with the splits.

I pray for patience and persistence for my children today. I know
their young eyes can see to the mountain summits, but they don't see
the valleys in between or the thousands of steps required to get to the
top. Bless their wonderful gifts of optimism and urgency; now begin to
season these gifts with clear thinking, hard work, and patience.

Lord, teach them to wait for You—through all the long, hot climbs
ahead. And not just to wait passively for Your magic wand to deliver the
success they want. Instead, instill in each one an attitude of *busy
waiting*. Each step of the climb is up to them; the final destination is up
to You (Prov. 19:21). Show me how to model this kind of active trust.

Along the way, help my children always to choose the proven path
of wisdom and hard work, not the dead end of a quick return for the
least effort. Clothe them with Your "power from on high," O Lord, so
they can be stars in life's biggest success stories: to love You and others
wholeheartedly, to bring You glory on earth, and to joyfully spread Your
gospel everywhere (Matt. 22:37-38; Luke 24:49; Acts 1:8).

And when the mountaintop is a long way off, encourage them by Your people and Your loving presence. During those waits, help my children to learn what You're trying to teach them. And no matter how slow things seem, help them to remember that even though You keep a different kind of clock (2 Pet. 3:8), Your will is being accomplished speedily (Ps. 147:15).

Because You are the God of time, may my children be strong, take courage, and wait with confidence today (Ps. 27:14). And when it comes time to put my child's name in lights, write this, O Lord: "He is blessed because he waited for me!" (from Isa. 30:18).

Amen.

Bad Company

He who walks [as a companion] with wise men is wise, but he
who associates with [self-confident] fools is [a fool himself and] shall
smart for it.

PROVERBS 13:20, AMP

PRAYING FROM PROVERBS

Lord,

Your Word is so clear on the dangers of the wrong crowd: "Do not envy
wicked men, do not desire their company" (24:1); "Do not join those
who drink too much wine" (23:20); "My son, if sinners entice you, do
not give in to them" (1:10).

I want to teach my children how to choose good friends, but I
need Your wisdom, Lord. Show me how to be a fair judge of character.
Help me to know when to let my children make their own decisions
about their companions and when I should intervene.

Enable my children to see through the surface appeal of all kinds of
lazy, dishonest, or dangerous people (1:10-19). So often these "sinners"
are portrayed as heroes and winners in music, film, and TV.

Lord, open my children's eyes to the truth. By Your grace, turn any
fascination with the wrong crowd into a holy zeal for loving and obeying You (23:17-18).

Amen.

Safe from Fear

For I am the LORD, your God, who takes hold of your right hand and says to you, Do not fear; I will help you.

ISAIAH 41:13

Heavenly Father,

Sometimes my children are troubled by fears. How well I remember wanting my father to be with me on days when I was scared of something. Wanting during fear-filled nights to be in the safest place on earth—sleeping safely right between Mom and Dad.

You understand how defenseless and small young ones can feel (Deut. 1:30-31). Help me to teach my children about the helping God who always holds their hands tightly (Isa. 41:13). May they experience for themselves what You have promised: "I will not in any way fail you nor give you up nor leave you without support. . . . [I will] not in any degree leave you helpless nor forsake nor . . . relax My hold on you!" (Heb. 13:5, AMP).

Teach my children to understand fear: how wise fear is so important but foolish fretting is so destructive (Prov. 22:3, Matt. 6:27); how running away from important confrontations can get us into trouble or deprive us of a big win (Jonah 1, Judges 6–7); how fear of the opinion of others is a waste of energy but fear of You, God, leads to blessing (Prov. 29:25).

May my children hear the voice of Jesus today saying, "Don't be afraid" (John 14:27). I look forward to the time when each child will learn to say with joy and confidence, "The Lord is my helper; I will not be afraid. What can man do to me?" (Heb. 13:6).

Amen.

Such Things As God Has Promised

P rayer, John Bunyan once said, "is a sincere, sensible, affectionate pouring out of the soul to God, through Christ in the strength and assistance of the Spirit, for such things as God has promised." Prayer, then, is more than our yearning for some personal benefit. It is our thoughtful and heartfelt response to a God who has already extended his hand of kindness to us.

BRUCE SHELLEY

PRAYER 12

Kneeling in My Heart

*Three times a day [Daniel] got down on his knees and prayed, giving
thanks to his God, just as he had done before.*

DANIEL 6:10

Lord,

Thank You that I can come into Your presence just as I am. You wait
patiently through my silences—and still welcome my prayers.

Help me to pray faithfully for my children. As much as I love
them, my record of praying for them is patchy at best. It's so much easier to pray for my own needs or not pray at all.

Lord, teach me to pray like Daniel, who, even under threat of being thrown to the lions, wouldn't stop talking to You. He held great
power in Babylon, yet Daniel knew the real power was Yours.

Help me to develop effective praying habits, whether these have to
do with time or place or method. Help me to carry in my heart all day
an attitude of kneeling on behalf of my children. I do kneel before You
now, God. You are king in my room right now, king in my life. And I
seize—with every fiber of faith in me—this fact: You are king in my
children's lives. Yours is the real power. You *will* reign! You *will* be glori-
fied! You *will* shut the lions' mouths. That's the kind of God You are.

By Your inner promptings, I will kneel in my heart all day with
thanksgiving and hope. And I'll remember this encouragement: "Trust
in him at all times, O people; pour out your hearts to him, for God is
our refuge" (Ps. 62:8).

Amen.

39

The Music of Loose Ends

Make music in your heart to the Lord, always giving thanks to God the Father for everything, in the name of our Lord Jesus Christ.

EPHESIANS 5:19-20

Heavenly Father,

You said "always." Always give thanks—always and for everything. You said to keep the music of thanksgiving always playing in my heart. Today, I give thanks in Jesus' name for what I usually complain about, for what I can't seem to control or change, for all the daily indignities of raising kids:

—For things that break or get broken all the time, and things that break on first use, and for the broken things that require expensive repair or replacement: Today I see that these are reminders that You are giving my family an eternal treasure in heaven that will never break or fade away (Matt. 6:20).

—For things stained, smudged, smeared, fingerprinted, spilled on, even for those unnameable stickynessess in strange places: Today I will bear with such messes with renewed patience because they remind me that it is the inside of us that matters. You have washed our hearts to purest white by the mercies of Your daily love and eternal salvation (Ps. 51:7).

—For things unemptied, unreplaced, unclosed, unreturned, unkempt, unfound, and unfinished: Today these loose ends of our family life reassure me that our family is called to a destiny where only a few things really matter (Luke 10:42).

—For things ugly, plain, common, cheap, chipped, and dented:

Today I see these sometimes-embarrassing belongings of a family for what they are—proof that a miracle is under way here. And You, Lord of all, choose to dwell here with us (Ps. 144:3).

—For noises day and night, and loud music, and loud noise that passes for music: Today I offer this racket to You as the praise of "everything that has breath" in this house (Ps. 150:6), and thank You with each decibel of devotion.

—For interrupted meals, unfinished conversations with friends, unfinished reading, neglected hobbies and projects, and for the fading memories of many small, grown-up luxuries: Today I remember that in His ministry, Jesus said that children were the most welcome interruption of all and the real business of heaven (Matt. 19:14).

O Father, accept my list of ordinary parenting annoyances as the holy music of my thankful heart today, for I sing in Jesus' name.

Amen.

Cruel World

I have thought deeply about all that goes on here in the world, where people have the power of injuring each other.

ECCLESIASTES 8:9, TLB

Lord,

Almost every day I hear terrible news on the radio—robberies, rapes, even the slaughter of innocent women and children. I find myself asking, Why does such evil seem to go unchecked? And why would I want to raise children in such a world?

Today I pray for understanding. How much I need Your help when my children's questions progress from "Why is the sky blue?" to "Why did that man hurt that little girl?" I confess, Lord, that their questions often echo my own. At times I cry out with Jeremiah, "Why do the wicked prosper? Why do the ones without faith live at ease?" (Jer. 12:1).

Thank You for hearing me out, for inviting all Your children to look for answers to the hard questions (Prov. 25:2). And in this process, help me remember to affirm for my children what I *know* to be true about You:

You, O Lord, are love (1 John 4:7-9). You are just and fair (Deut. 32:4). You are good and merciful to all (Nah. 1:7, 2 Pet. 3:9). You have the power to accomplish anything (Jer. 32:17). You care for Your own (Psalm 23). You are ultimately in control (Ps. 146:10). You *will* bring the wicked to justice, and You *will* comfort the oppressed (Jer. 9:24).

Thank You that our family can count on You in a sometimes cruel and frightening world. Though evil threatens, You still hold our family in Your hands. Help us rest in Your care today.

Amen.

Sweet Obedience

Children, obey your parents in the Lord, for this is right.

EPHESIANS 6:1

Heavenly Father,
You know what it's like to want to have children who obey You. You discipline us and give us guidelines for our own good and because of Your great love for us (Heb.12:6).

May I share this motivation of Yours when I ask my children to obey. Lord, let my kids see that I obey You because I love You.

Your Word says not only is it right for children to obey their parents (Eph. 6:1) but also that it will go better with them all their lives if they do (Eph. 6:3). And, yes, it will go better for me, too. But I also pray that my kids will *want* to obey—not only for me, or to avoid trouble, but because it pleases You (Col. 3:20).

Make me a good example of obedience, Lord. Show me if I am doing anything to discourage or dishearten my children (Eph. 6:4), such as being inconsistent, inattentive, harsh, or plain old crabby. After all, I know it is Your kindness that leads us to repentance, not Your threats of punishment (Rom. 2:4).

Amen.

My Kids Are Conquerors!

In all these things we are more than conquerors through him who loved us.

ROMANS 8:37

PRAYING FROM ROMANS 8

Lord,

Today I pray with joy and relief the apostle Paul's inspiring words to the Roman believers.

How I thank You that You stand ready to make every turn of events work together for good for my children if they're following You (v. 28).

Before my children were born, You planned for them to be saved and also to become more and more like You as they grow and mature (v. 29). By Your power You are even now bringing this glorious plan to life—guaranteeing it, making it possible, and making it work—on a daily basis. All the important stuff is really up to You (v. 30).

What can I say in response?

What a relief! If You, Lord, are this much on my kids' side, if You're working this way on their behalf every day, who or what can really get in the way of Your awesome plan for their lives (v. 31)?

How often I pray fervently for my children, pleading with You for their lives—sometimes as if I'm trying to convince You to notice or love them. How could I ever dream of not trusting You with them when You gave up Your one and only Son for their sake (v. 32)?

And if You would give up Jesus, Your Son, to pay the price for my children's lives, how could I imagine that You would not freely give them anything they need to hold fast to what You've bought for them (v. 32)? If You have saved them, who can unsave them? Even when my kids sin terribly, who can successfully condemn them when Your own Son now defends them personally (vv. 33-34)?

You know me, Lord. I've imagined every possible thing that could go wrong in the lives of my children. Every disaster or hardship. Even the threat that terrible persecution could somehow rise up in our country (vv. 35-36).

But no matter which of these scary possibilities I point to, my kids are more than conquerors through You (v. 37)! To be *more than* a conqueror must mean that there is hardly a struggle. On these truths, there *is* no contest. What You have secured for my kids from before time can't be trifled with now by anyone or anything (vv. 38-39).

I'm convinced. I'd be a fool to think for even a moment that anything in the world could separate my children from You (v. 39). *Nothing*—war, drugs, serious mistakes, bad grades, accidents, evil people, poverty, illness, or even death—can come between my children and Your all-powerful love.

Thank You, Lord, that ultimately this truth is all that really matters. What if hard times come or we starve or the boogieman turns out to be real or Martians really do exist?

"Go ahead," I can say with confidence. "Make God's day. But be warned . . . my kids are more than conquerors through Him."

Amen.

A Listening Prayer

The LORD confides in those who fear him; he makes his covenant known to them. My eyes are ever on the LORD.

PSALM 25:14-15

Lord Jesus,
Today, I wait for You.
Give me eyes to see only You
and ears to hear only You.

I lay aside every worry about my kids,
every request for them.
I keep for myself only this:
    Your willingness to speak to us.

I hold You in awe, my God.
You are too high, too great for me,
yet in David's psalm today
    You promise to confide in me.

Yes, Lord, please make Your desires known to me
and to my dear children today.
I hold up each one before You now.
I will treasure what You tell me
and obey with all my heart.

    What is it that You are trying to say, Lord?

A Loving Gaze, Constantly Fixed

There is not in the world a life more pleasing and more delicious than a life of continual conversation with God; only those can understand it who practice and experience it. If I were a preacher, I would preach above everything else the practice of the presence of God. I strive only to dwell in His holy presence, and do that by a simple attention and loving gaze constantly fixed upon Him, which I am able to call a real presence of God; or to say it better, a secret conversation, silent and habitual, of the soul with God.

FROM THE LETTERS OF BROTHER LAWRENCE

The Great Escape

We have escaped like a bird out of the fowler's snare.

PSALM 124:7

PRAYING FROM PSALM 124

If You, O Lord,
had not been on our side
   (I'm praying for the whole family when I say this)
if You had not been on our side:
    —when ear infections, rashes, night sweats, colic, scary concussions, high fevers, broken bones, multiple stitches, and all sorts of growing-up owies came our way;
    —when suspicious intruders, preoccupied baby-sitters, careless medical staff, neighborhood troublemakers, misinformed teachers, unhelpful relatives, and all sorts of people hazards came our way;
    —when disappointing church experiences, boring devotions, absent-minded praying, bad examples from other believers, and all sorts of spiritual disasters-in-the-making came our way;
    —when car crunches and near misses, bad tempers and forgotten resolutions, mixed-up prescriptions and quarrelsome vacation trips, tiny lies and terrible divorces, wrong-spirited discipline and empty-headed decisions and all sorts of family failures came our way . . .

If You had not been on our side, O gracious Lord—
   Our little family would have been swallowed alive by now!
   The deluge of troubles would have swept us away!

Yes, when we think of the enemies of our family, we have one relieved response today:

"Praise be to the LORD, . . .

> We have escaped like a bird out of the fowler's snare;
> the snare has been broken, and we have escaped.
> Our help is in the name of the LORD, the Maker of heaven and
> earth." (vv. 6-8)

> Amen.

Enter, Spirit

The Spirit gives life; the flesh counts for nothing. The words I have spoken to you are spirit and they are life.

JOHN 6:63

Lord,

Today I pray that Your Spirit will live in each of my children. Make my children part of Your kingdom—not through rules but through right-eousness, peace, and joy in Your Holy Spirit (Rom. 14:17).

From birth, we're so stuck in "flesh" (Ps. 51:5): schedules, aches, nagging worries, pride, and our silly human way of limiting You. Give us life, O Spirit! Free us from sin and doubt and distraction. Help our whole family to sing Your song all day. Let us pour forth—as Your other created things do (Ps. 8:1; 19:2)—the praises of God.

Lord, let Your Holy Spirit enter here, by every door, every impulse. Let my children's every turning be toward You. Be pleased to dwell in our home in fullness so that we will always be in step with You (Gal. 5:25). Anoint our conversation with grace. Season our humor with kindness. Nudge us to serve. Compel us to be grateful for everything.

Through this prayer of faith, release Your rivers of living water to flow out of my children today (John 7:38).

Amen.

An Honest Heart

*Whoever can be trusted with very little can also be trusted with much,
and whoever is dishonest with very little will also be dishonest with
much.*

LUKE 16:10

Lord, Spirit of Truth,
All parents want to think that their children are honest and that they
would never lie to them. When we discover that one of our kids has
deceived us—perhaps with a bold-faced lie—we are devastated.

You know what that's like, Lord. You, too, desire truth in the core
of our being (Ps. 51:6). And yet You also know that our hearts are de-
ceitful above all things (Jer. 17:9).

Lord, wickedness and lying are rampant everywhere my kids turn
(Ps. 12:2). Others cheat on tests for A's, their friends lie to their parents,
and even *I* have been known to treat a "white lie" as if it didn't count.

Help my children to see that if they are dishonest in the little
things, they will end up being dishonest in big things. And if they can
be trusted with something as small as their lunch money now, someday
they will be trusted with much more (Matt. 25:21).

Help my children to feel Your delight when they speak the truth
and to remember that You hate it when we lie (Prov. 12:22). And when
they persevere toward truth, may they feel great freedom of spirit (John
8:32)—so much so that the passing reward of a lie looks as cheap and
fleeting as it really is.

In Your name I pray. Amen.

The Bread of Life

My soul will be satisfied as with the richest of foods.

PSALM 63:5

Lord,

I need Your strength today. Sometimes it feels like a full-time job just to keep all the mouths in this family fed. My kids think about food day and night—in the car, at the movies, after they've gone to bed.

Why spend money on what is not bread, and your labor on what does not satisfy? Listen, listen to me, and eat what is good, and your soul will delight in the richest of fare (Isa. 55:2).

I believe You, Lord. Help me as I prepare meals or shop for food to keep remembering how much my kids also need spiritual nourishment. Create in them an intense soul-hunger along with a growing understanding that only You can satisfy their need.

Man shall not live on bread alone, but on every word that proceeds out of the mouth of God (Matt. 4:4, NASB).

Yes, Lord. Your words are the nourishment my family needs most. I want to hand out Your words like midday snacks. Help me to serve Your promises like lavish meals and keep Your commandments as close at hand as staples in our pantry. Help me find ways to keep the spiritual fridge in this house full of food and drink at all times.

Whoever drinks the water I give him will never thirst. Indeed, the water I give him will become in him a spring of water welling up to eternal life (John 4:14).

Thank You, Lord, that it's not all up to me. You alone can give my child an endless stream of life and nourishment that is always available to satisfy a famished spirit. Lord, help each of my children to find this source of new life.

I am the living bread that came down from heaven. If anyone eats of this bread, he will live forever. This bread is my flesh, which I will give for the life of the world (John 6:51).

Lord, You not only provide us with spiritual food, You *are* spiritual food! You gave Your life to satisfy our spiritual hunger. Help my children to hunger and thirst for You so that they will seek You out. And guide me as I try to convey the urgency of this quest—because they will literally die if they don't partake of You.

Whoever eats my flesh and drinks my blood remains in me, and I in him (John 6:56).

Thank You for Your promise that if my children make You their true food and drink, You will take it upon Yourself to keep them close to You. Lord, especially when our family participates in the sacrament of Communion, may we remember You with sincere gratitude.

Amen.

Boy Meets Girl

When Jacob saw Rachel daughter of Laban, his mother's brother, and Laban's sheep, he went over and rolled the stone away from the mouth of the well and watered his uncle's sheep.

Lord,

You created us male and female, and together we somehow complete the picture of who You are (Gen. 5:1-2). No wonder my children are fascinated with all things involving that other gender! And no wonder Jacob was so anxious to help out beautiful Rachel.

Thank You that You not only created the abiding love of marriage (Gen. 2:24), but You also understand crushes, puppy love, and the passing storms of teen romance.

Today I pray that You would help my children develop healthy and rewarding relationships with members of the opposite sex throughout their lives. How much I will need Your help as notes passed in elementary school progress to flirting in the halls and then to phone calls and—how will I cope?—serious dating!

Lord, help my children begin with the basics of opposite-sex relationships. May they learn how to show respect, use good manners, and express genuine interest in others. Help them to become comfortable just talking and laughing with friends of the other gender.

As my kids begin to "go out" with a boy or a girl, help them be wise about their level of emotional intimacy. Help them develop healthy habits of communication within their friendships. And help them not to get too serious too soon.

Please protect them from heartbreak, Lord! And if pain or rejection comes, please use it to teach my children important lessons about life and love (2 Cor. 6:14-17). Lord, I pray that my children would refuse to be involved with a boyfriend or girlfriend who doesn't love You (v. 14).

Right now I pray for the husbands or wives that my children, if they marry, will spend their lives with. Bring each couple together in Your perfect way. Have Your hand on them even now. And may their eventual commitment to marriage be strong enough to stand up against any trouble or testing life brings.

While they're growing up, introduce them to couples who are good examples of how beautiful married love is meant to be.

In the meantime, may all of their boy-girl friendships continue to be a source of healthy fun, bringing them new insight into themselves and others. May their whispers and glances and blushes help to prepare them for a happy future. And may they praise You and thank You for the marvelous gift of male and female.

Amen.

A Blessing for Freedom

ecause you, _____, are a follower of Jesus, I bless you in His powerful and beautiful name. May the truth of His teachings set you free from everything that could hold you captive today. By Christ's power, be free to become all He wants you to be!

FROM JOHN 8:31-32

Three Freedoms

You will know the truth, and the truth will set you free.

JOHN 8:32

MEDITATIONS TO CARRY THROUGH THE DAY

O Lord,
In my heart today I will try to prize only those truths that set me and my family free. Show me practical ways to encourage my children with these meditations—a note in a lunchbox or under a pillow, a message left on an answering machine, a grace said at the table. May these meditations become the credo of each child in this house, a constant reassurance of our family's true identity.

    Amen.

I am a child of light. (Eph. 5:8)
I am clothed with Jesus Christ. (Rom. 13:14)
I am surrounded by his favor like a shield. (Ps. 5:12)

or

_____ is a child of light.
_____ is clothed with Jesus Christ.
_____ is surrounded by Your favor like a shield.

Watch Over My Child

*When she saw that he was a fine child, she hid him for three months.
But when she could hide him no longer, she got a papyrus basket for him
and coated it with tar and pitch. Then she placed the child in it and put
it among the reeds along the bank of the Nile.*

EXODUS 2:2-3

Heavenly Father,

How great and mysterious are Your ways! You ask us to trust You with
that which we love most. How did Moses' mother do it? How did she
let her baby go, knowing so many things could go wrong?

The dangers my children face today are very different, Lord, and
yet just as real. Drugs, strangers, household accidents, gangs—even bad
baby-sitters!

Thank You that even when my children are out of my sight, they
are *never* out of Your sight. Please watch over them in all they do and
through every encounter they have with the world.

Thank You that I can surrender my child and place him in the
dangerous river of life, knowing that You will be watching over him,
not from far off but from very nearby.

Amen.

A Long and Happy Life

My son, do not forget my teaching, but keep my commands in your heart, for they will prolong your life many years and bring you prosperity.

PROVERBS 3:1-2

PRAYING PROVERBS 3:1-8

Heavenly Father,

I pray today that You will bless my children with long and happy lives. Help them to treasure Your Word deep in their hearts so it influences and directs their every choice and desire (v. 1). As they mature, show them how those who make wrong choices—even if they're famous or rich—so often end up ruined or unhappy (v. 2).

I pray that my children will put a high priority on love and faithfulness, exhibiting them like beautiful clothing or jewelry. Show them how to make these qualities part of their personalities so they will win the favor of the right people and, above all, please You (vv. 3-4).

Guide my children to trust You with their whole hearts—all their minds, all their wills, all their hopes. And help them to keep a healthy caution about the reliability of their own "wisdom" (vv. 5-7).

As they affirm You as Lord in their choices, make the way ahead plain for them (v. 6). As they honor You and despise evil, bring them health, peace, and prosperity (vv. 7-8).

Amen.

God Is For Me

If you do your duty and are punished for it and can still accept it patiently, you are doing something worthwhile in God's sight.

1 PETER 2:20, PH

Lord Jesus,

No one knows better than You what it is like to be misunderstood or treated unfairly. You warned us that everyone who wants to live a godly life in harmony with Yours will be persecuted (2 Tim. 3:12).

This is a difficult truth, especially when I consider my children. Kids can be so hard on one another. I pray that when my children are mocked, abused, or maligned for saying or doing what is right, they will come to You for comfort and help (Ps. 34:8).

Show my children what it means to rejoice in trials and tribulations for Your sake (James 1:2-3). May they speak up for, and live for, You. When they face teasing or opposition from their peers, help my children to remember the words, "God is for me!" (Ps. 56:9).

May my children learn not to return insult for insult but to do what is harder instead: to pay back with a blessing (1 Pet. 3:9). Thank You that when my children suffer for doing right, You will in turn bless them! (1 Pet. 2:20).

Amen.

Love Is . . .

If I speak in the tongues of men and of angels, but have not love, I am only a resounding gong or a clanging cymbal.

1 CORINTHIANS 13:1

PRAYING FROM 1 CORINTHIANS 13:4-8

Heavenly Father,

How easy it is for parents to become clanging cymbals in the ears of their kids! I feel that I love my children so much it breaks my heart some days. But You remind me that love is more than emotion. It's possible for me to discipline, to teach, and even to provide—all without love.

Today I pray that none of my efforts will be wasted because every aspect of my parenting is backed up by the true qualities of love:

When I feel tense and short-tempered, help me to take a deep breath and remember that love is patient (v. 4).

When I am wrapped up in my own to-do lists, remind me to take time to pay attention and be kind to my children (v. 4).

When I am tempted to compare my kids with other people's kids, help me to remember that genuine love doesn't express itself through envying—or boasting, either (v. 4).

When I discipline or reprimand my kids, help me to check my tone of voice and my expression, remembering that love is not rude (v. 5).

When my kids argue, beg, or whine, remind me that love is always slow to anger (v. 5).

When I'm at my wit's end and tempted to give my kids a quick rundown of all the things they've done wrong the past few days to bring me to this point, remind me that love doesn't keep a record of wrongs (v. 5).

When I feel twinges of smugness about another parent's failure, remind me that love doesn't rejoice over bad news but when good happens (v. 6).

When I'm ready to take a foolish risk with my child's safety because I'm too distracted or too tired to insist on precautions, remind me that love always protects (v. 7).

When I'm reluctant to let my child take on challenges he seems ready for, remind me to trust You and what You're doing in my child (v. 7).

When I'm discouraged about my child's progress in a certain area, remind me that love always hopes, even in the face of setbacks (v. 7).

When I'm tired and feeling like I just can't parent well, remind me that love never gives up (v. 7).

How I thank You, Lord, for the power of love in action. Thank You that if I parent with love and by the power of Your Spirit, I cannot fail (v. 8).

Amen.

Prayer for a Daughter

I am sending you out like sheep among wolves. Therefore be as shrewd as snakes and as innocent as doves.

MATTHEW 10:16

Lord,

You've blessed my daughter _____ with a sweet, guileless, and giving nature. What a gift she is to our family!

She's a tender lamb, a harmless dove, but look at the world we're in, Lord Jesus! My prayer today is that You would keep her spirit from hurt and harm. Mature her so that her tenderness doesn't render her gullible or foolish (Hos. 7:11). Underneath her sweet exterior, make her astute and perceptive (Matt. 10:16).

Bless her with a beautiful strength, a wise innocence, a shielded vulnerability (1 Pet. 3:4-5). How much You could nurture, heal, comfort, and encourage others through such gifts, Lord!

Bring her a husband in Your time who will cherish her, honor her, and protect her for exactly these wonderful qualities.

For her whole life, I claim these truths for her from Psalm 91:

You will be her true dwelling place and refuge (vv. 1-2); under Your wings she will find covering and comfort (v. 4); You will save her from terrors and fears (v. 5); You will protect her from physical and spiritual diseases (v. 6); You will give Your angels power to guard her (vv. 11-13); You will answer her when she calls, because You love her (v. 15).

Yes, Lord, You will always treasure her even more than I do. I thank You and bless You!

Amen.

God Loves What Is Not Yet

od loves what in us is not yet. What has still to come to birth. God, loving what is not yet and putting faith in us, continually begets us, since love is what begets. By giving us confidence, God helps us to be born, since love is what helps us to emerge from our darkness and draws us to the light. And this is such a fine thing to do that God invites us to do the same. The charity which God transmits to us is this very ability to love things in a person which do not as yet exist.

CARLO CARRETTO

Precious in My Eyes

You are precious in my eyes and I love you.

FROM ISAIAH 43:4

O Great, All-Seeing Lord,
You know me completely—and I'm still precious in Your eyes! Before my children have a thought, a feeling, or an intention, You understand it completely, and You welcome them into Your lap (Ps. 139:1-4, Luke 18:16). Thank You, loving God. Because You look on us with compassion, we can expect a lifetime of hope and help (Ps. 103:13,17).

I want to see my children as You do today. You looked with compassion on the self-centered, demanding crowds that hounded You like paparazzi during Your ministry (Matt. 9:36). While we were still sinners and busy rejecting You, You looked on the human race and saw only people worth dying for (Rom. 5:8).

Today where I see repeated failure, give me Your eyes to see a child who's not ready yet for what I'd like him to do.

Where I see disobedience, give me Your eyes to see an opportunity to positively affect his future with compassion and discipline.

Where I see only squabbling, give me Your eyes to see competitive, strong-minded children who will grow up to strive for great things.

Where I see only a family in shambles, give me Your eyes to see an exciting construction zone for human beings You love without reservation—one of whom is me (John 15:12-14).

Amen.

Prayer for a Son

I am sending to you Timothy, my son whom I love.

1 CORINTHIANS 4:17

Holy, Loving Father,
I join with the apostle Paul today in earnest prayer for my
son, _____.

Teach him how to enjoy his youth, without worrying if others look
down on him because he's still learning. Even now, may he set an
example for others in speech, in life, in love, in faith, and in purity
(1 Tim. 4:12).

Help him value godliness more than fitness or appearance. May he
learn that godliness holds promise for both the present life and the life
to come (4:8).

Show him how to keep himself pure (5:22), highly prizing a clean
conscience (1:19).

I pray that he would see through—and reject—godless myths, no
matter how popular or how many of his peers embrace them (4:7).
Help him to pursue more than money with his talents; may he pursue
instead the wealth that comes from righteousness, godliness, faith, love,
endurance, and gentleness (6:11).

Help my son, Father, to fight the good fight of the faith. May he
treasure the eternal destiny to which he was called when he confessed
You as Lord (6:12).

Amen.

The Daily Basics

So do not worry, saying, "What shall we eat?" or "What shall we drink?"
. . . your heavenly Father knows that you need them. . . . Until now you
have not asked for anything in my name. Ask and you will receive, and
your joy will be complete.

MATTHEW 6:31-32; JOHN 16:24

Heavenly Father,
You see the threats to our future, the low bank account, the worn relationships, the insipid busyness that passes for family life, the empty
cupboards of our hearts. And You love us! You will never turn us away
because of our inadequacies or our needs.

Today I pray for our needs, based on what You have already
told me.

—You told me to ask rather than worry, and You would give (Matt.
6:31-32). In Your presence, I acknowledge each physical need for my
children. I ask for food, health, clothing, and shelter for them.

—You told me that You could meet all of my children's spiritual
needs through the incomparable resources available in Christ Jesus
(Phil. 4:19). Right now I ask for protection, good friends, the strength
to make good choices, the perseverance that growing up takes.

—You told me that when we ask in Your name, our needs will be
met and our hearts will be joyful (John 16:23-24). So I dare to present
these needs to You as an act of worship—a way of declaring that only
You understand our true needs and only You can meet them fully.

Amen.

The Right Response

My son, if sinners entice you, do not give in to them.

PROVERBS 1:10

Holy Spirit,

Thank You that Your goodness is powerfully present in my children's lives. Today I pray that You will intervene when others who are driven by evil desires try to lure my children into doing wrong. Open my children's eyes to recognize troublemakers for what they are: rebels who live without Your blessing (Prov. 3:33).

Start now, God, to make my children smart beyond their years (Ps. 119:99). As my children are growing up, there will be many times when they meet those who are pursuing sin and who will make a strong case for my children to join in. Help them choose the right response quickly, without toying with a bad idea. May they say with David, "Away from me, you wrongdoers! I want to keep the commands of my God!" (Ps. 119:115).

And if things are getting out of hand, protect them from evil by Your power, God (Ps. 121:7); at key moments hide them from those who are too strong for them (Ps. 31:20).

Help me to teach my children the truth about wrongdoers:

—They get caught in the traps they set for others (Prov. 1:18).

—They lose what they already have when they take from others (Prov. 2:22).

—They try to be smart or "cool," but their foolishness will lead them toward trouble and death (Prov. 5:22-23).

Thank You, Holy Spirit, that You are my child's Protector.

Amen.

Story Man

Now when he saw the crowds, he went up on a mountainside and sat down. His disciples came to him, and he began to teach them.

MATTHEW 5:1-2

A FAMILY PRAYER

Jesus, friend of ordinary moms and dads and story man for boys and girls, be our dearest houseguest today. (Have mercy on our messes.)

I will come and make my home in your heart (from John 14:23). We want to wait on You with extravagance.

Your sins are forgiven because you love Me much (from Luke 7:47). Please tell us Your stories about seeds and coins and nail prints.

The words I speak are spirit and they are life (from John 6:63). We will watch Your eyes. We will remember Your voice and the smell of salt air . . .

Follow me! (John 21:19). We will give You our fish-and-bread lunch. We will share our tree fort and our berry punch.

I am the bread of life. You will never go hungry (from John 6:35). We will scribble Your name—*Jesus is Lord!*—in our Day-Timer or whisper it over laundry.

If you keep quiet, the stones will cry out! (from Luke 19:40). And when we turn in at night, please forgive us if we're too tired to remember all the stories You told us today.

Come to me, . . . and I will give you rest (Matt 11:28). In heaven and on earth, You are all we desire, Jesus.

Amen.

A Blessing for a Cloudy Day

ay our Lord Jesus Christ himself and God our Father, who loved us and by His grace gave us eternal encouragement and good hope, encourage your hearts and strengthen you in every good deed and word.

2 THESSALONIANS 2:16-17

Cloudy Day

Why are you downcast, O my soul? Why so disturbed within me? Put your hope in God, for I will yet praise him, my Savior and my God.

PSALM 42:11

Lord Jesus,

It's cloudy here today. I sense overcast feelings, heavy thoughts, a drizzle of discouragement in myself and my kids. Right now, for all of us, I lift our dim thoughts and feelings to You, Light of the World.

Do not let your hearts be troubled. Trust in . . . Me (John 14:1).

Lord, You went through this. As a child, You slogged through drab days. As a man, You held on through storms of anguish and tears. You were made like us in every way so that You could become our merciful and faithful high priest (Heb. 2:17).

Don't let your happy trust in Me die away, no matter what happens. Remember your reward (from Heb. 10:35, TLB).

How I thank You, Lord, that on days just like this You take my children's burdens on Yourself so they don't have to carry them (Matt. 11:28). Thank You that no matter how unappealing our emotions are, You're always at work, renewing us day by day (2 Cor. 4:16).

I am the God of hope. Let Me fill you with joy and peace so that you may overflow with the power of My Holy Spirit (from Rom. 15:13).

Lord, because of who You are, today can be a good day. I trust You.

My redeemed one, soon you will be singing! (from Isa. 51:11).

Amen.

Such Is the Kingdom

[Jesus] said to them, "Let the children come to me, for the Kingdom of God belongs to such as they. Don't send them away! I tell you as seriously as I know how that anyone who refuses to come to God as a little child will never be allowed into his Kingdom."

Then he took the children into his arms and placed his hands on their heads and he blessed them.

MARK 10:14-16, TLB

Dear Lord Jesus,

Open the eyes of my spirit to see this scene on a Judean hillside: anxious mothers, grumpy disciples, wide-eyed toddlers stumbling around Your feet. And You, Lord, interrupting everything to sweep a child into Your arms.

Today I pray that my children will know that they are treasured by You. Forgive me when I don't want to be bothered, when I inadvertently "send them away" from You.

Help my children—even as they can't wait to grow up—to hang on to the childlike qualities You celebrate. Teach them how to cling to simplicity, faith, a trusting heart. And remind them that they are always welcome on Your lap.

Lord, I'm in an ordinary house and not on a hillside. But I bring You my children. Please take them in Your arms, put Your gentle hands on their heads, and bless them. Thank You!

Amen.

Doing Is Believing

Little children, let us stop just saying we love people; let us really love them, and show it by our actions.

1 JOHN 3:18, TLB

Lord,

It is so much easier to say, "Just do it!" than to actually pull on our sweats. Or to say, "I love you" than to be loving when it's hard. Today I pray that my children will be doers of love, not just hearers and talkers (James 1:22).

May the events of this day help each child see that all the good deeds and right beliefs in the world are lifeless if they're not backed up by actions (James 2:20). Help us to be a doing family today—whether it's by finishing tasks, volunteering to help, or simply treating each other as we want to be treated (Matt. 7:12).

You have given each of us so many gifts to share (1 Pet. 4:10)—but we get careless and selfish. Show my children how to put them to work for You. Especially I pray about this for _____ right now. How I long for a lifestyle of obedience and goodness for each of my children!

Lord, give my children Your strength to act when they are tired or unmotivated (Phil. 2:13). Help them not to become weary in doing good but to trust You to reward their efforts in Your time (Gal. 6:9).

And let every little deed be a love gift to You today.

Amen.

Full of Confidence

My eyes stay open . . . that I may meditate on your promises.

PSALM 119:148

MEDITATIONS TO CARRY THROUGH THE DAY

I'm confident of this,
that God, who began a good work in my child, _____ ,
will carry it on to completion until the
day of Christ Jesus.
(from Phil.1:6)

Here is a trustworthy saying:
If _____ is faithless,
God will remain faithful.
(2 Tim. 2:11,13)

Singing in Bed

Sing to the LORD a new song. . . . For the LORD takes delight in his people; he crowns the humble with salvation. Let the saints rejoice in this honor and sing for joy on their beds.

PSALM 149:1,4-5

O Lord of my nights,
Your delight in my family is all around me, even at night. We're healthy, safe, warm, and fed. You've surrounded my children with a world of small beauties and large mysteries.

You have invited us into Your special family; our new life in You is a priceless gift. Thank You for the way You're drawing each family member—in different ways—into a deeper relationship with You. I know that You will never give up on this work of salvation in each of us.

I delight in this honor today. We're in no way worthy of all Your goodness, but You are in every way worthy of our praise!

At bedtime or during the night when those quiet moments come, help me lead each of my children in his or her own expression of love to You. During those moments turn our thoughts away from our little troubles.

And during my nights—whether I'm half-asleep, in a knot of worry, or just staring into the darkness—may I sing new songs of joy, joy to You, Lord of my nights!

Amen.

Ten Keys to a Good Life

Keep his decrees and commands . . . so that it may go well with you and your children after you.

DEUTERONOMY 4:40

PRAYING THE TEN COMMANDMENTS

Lord God,

You asked us to write Your commands in our memories and affections (Deut. 6:6) and to impress them on our children's hearts and minds. Show our family today, Lord, what it means to fear You and keep Your laws so that we receive the best life has to offer (Deut 7:12).

1. "I am the LORD your God, who brought you out of . . . slavery. You shall have no other gods before me" (Deut. 5:6-7). May no other loyalties or affections take Your place in my children's hearts—no other priority, hobby, ambition, possession, or person. We belong to only You!

2. "You shall not make for yourself an idol in the form of anything in heaven above or on the earth. . . . You shall not . . . worship them; for I . . . am a jealous God" (vv. 8-9). May my children resist any substitute objects of worship and turn away from all false beliefs. Keep my children from any pursuit—no matter how worthy—that becomes an end in itself.

3. "You shall not misuse the name of the LORD your God" (v. 11). Help us to treasure and protect Your name, O Lord. In a casually profane world, keep my children sensitive about the sacredness of Your names, especially "Lord," "God," and "Jesus Christ."

4. "Observe the Sabbath day by keeping it holy" (v. 12). May my

children set aside the Lord's Day for worship and rest and for nurturing a vital role in Your church family. Thank You for setting us free from the tyranny of work and "getting ahead."

5. "Honor your father and your mother, as the LORD your God has commanded you, so that you may live long and that it may go well with you" (v. 16). May our children respect and obey us as their main source for learning about life and godliness—even when we are aging and weak. And may You bless them as a result.

6. "You shall not murder" (v. 17). Help my children to revere the sanctity of all human life—including unborn or aged. And beginning now, may my children never surrender to hate, violence, or vengeance.

7. "You shall not commit adultery" (v. 18). May my children build their relationships on integrity, purity, faithfulness, and loyalty. Protect them from pornography and promiscuity. Teach them to honor marriage as a sacred, lifelong commitment.

8. "You shall not steal" (v. 19). May my children learn early to respect the belongings of others, to value honesty, and to trust You, our Provider, to take care of their wants and needs.

9. "You shall not give false testimony against your neighbor" (v. 20). Instill in my children a sincere dedication to the truth and to defending the needs of the weak.

10. "You shall not covet" (v. 21). Help my children never to measure themselves by the lives or possessions of others. Instead, may they be content with what You give and be happy when others prosper.

Lord God, thank You for Your gracious promise to bless us and our children if we follow these laws (Deut. 7:12). We want Your covenant of love to be the measure of our lives.

Amen.

My Child's Shepherd

He maketh me to lie down in green pastures: he leadeth me beside the still waters.

PSALM 23:2, KJV

PRAYING PSALM 23

Lord,

You are my child's Shepherd. Because her care is Your personal concern, she will never be without anything she truly needs (v. 1).

Please lead her, today and every day, into places and experiences where her soul will be revived and her spiritual passion will be continually restored (vv. 2-3).

When daily life weighs her down or the fear of death somehow casts a shadow over her spirit, make Your loving presence known to her. By Your own hand carry her along, comfort her, and nudge her toward maturity (v. 4).

In her times of crisis, surrounded perhaps by those who want and expect her to fail, come through for her, God. Display Your lavish affection for her. Prove to all that she is Your chosen one, the apple of Your eye, and that You have nothing but overflowing blessings in store for her (v. 5).

Yes, Lord, may Your unfailing goodness and tender mercies surround her all the days of her life, and may she find her true home in Your presence forever (v. 6).

Amen.

A Cheerful Face

A happy heart makes the face cheerful, but heartache crushes the spirit.

PROVERBS 15:13

Lord,

When I see my child in the dumps, I remember that You are a Lord of compassion. You took our weaknesses upon Yourself, and You carried our sorrows (Isa. 53:3-4). How I thank You, loving Lord of sad children, that You feel my child's heartache, too!

When I long to see my child's face happy again, show me how to talk with him; help me listen well. Is there worry? Is there fear? Are others bringing grief to my child? Is there hidden wrongdoing? Or is this discouragement a passing thing?

Give me the kind of wise insight that only comes from You (James 1:5). Help me be a healer to my child, bringing cheer with kind words and tender touches (Prov. 12:25). By Your Spirit, turn these times into opportunities to teach my child this wonderful promise: Be of good courage, and God will strengthen your heart (Ps. 31:24).

In Your name I pray. Amen.

To Love Your Word

My heart is set on keeping your decrees to the very end.

PSALM 119:112

PRAYING FROM PSALM 119

Lord,

Today I pray that you will open my children's eyes to the truths of the Bible; may they find and experience the wonders of your Word (v. 18). I pray this for myself and especially for my child, _____.

Teach my children to follow Your rules for living throughout their whole lives (v. 33). Give them a spiritual understanding of the Bible—deeper than awareness or knowledge or even memory—that will help them wholeheartedly obey it (v. 34).

Lead them clearly and firmly in the path of Your teachings (v. 35). Use Your Word to show them what to do in small and large decisions. Let Bible truths help them find the way home when problems are too big for them (v. 130).

Draw my children into a sincere love for Your Word; deliver them from shortsighted, selfish living (v. 36). Please, Lord, let the blazing wonder of Your truths turn my children's eyes away from wanting what is worthless in the long run. And keep renewing their passion for You (v. 37).

Amen.

Footrace

In a race all the runners run, but only one gets the prize. Run in such a way as to get the prize.

1 CORINTHIANS 9:24

Lord,
You know very well that my children are in a contest today. In this race, however, speed doesn't count for much, and trophies won't be handed out for a long time.

The stands are mostly full of witnesses from another world (1 Tim. 6:12). But You are also there, cheering on all of my children. And it is You alone, Lord, who give them confidence and keep their feet from slipping (Prov. 3:23).

Give my children faith and strength to continue the contest of life each day. Help them to run their race well, to throw off and set aside anything—bad habits, temptations, laziness—that might get in their way (Heb. 12:1). Help them live in such a way that they win!

May my children realize that knowing You is the only prize in life that matters. Everything else is like garbage (Phil. 3:8). Today help all of us in our family to compete for You with every fiber of our being!

Amen.

Safe and Sound

He has saved me from death, my eyes from tears, my feet from stumbling.
I shall live! Yes, in his presence—here on earth!

PSALM 116:8-9, TLB

PRAYING PSALM 116

Wonderful Lord,

I love You because You listen to me when I cry out to You for mercy, no
matter how desperate, redundant, or scared I sound (v. 1).

How many times You've heard me praying when I feared for my
child's safety—in the car, in unsafe neighborhoods, late at night, with
untrustworthy friends, in dangerous sports, on a bed of illness. Lord,
You understand how troubled and anxious I can become for my children. Death could so easily snatch them away (v. 3)!

But You've heard me wailing, "O Lord, preserve _____'s life"
(v. 4). You have always shown me Your kindness. You are full of compassion toward me and my kids (v. 5). You watch over Your little ones.
When we are in great need, You rescue us (v. 6).

How can I repay You, Lord, for Your goodness to us (v. 12)? I will
tell others about Your power to save (v. 13). I will keep the promises I've
made to You concerning me and my children (v. 14). Thank You for
Your faithfulness to us.

Amen.

A Psalm of Love

Thank you for children brought into being because we loved. God of love, keep us loving so that they may grow up whole in love's over-flow.

JOE BAYLY

The Gift of Grandparents

So Boaz took Ruth and she became his wife. Then he went to her, and the LORD enabled her to conceive, and she gave birth to a son. The women said to Naomi: "Praise be to the LORD, who this day has not left you without a kinsman-redeemer. . . . He will renew your life and sustain you in your old age.

RUTH 4:13-15

Blessed Savior,

Today I pray that You would help my children learn the importance of extended family, especially Grandma and Grandpa.

I know my kids don't always grasp the value of grandparents, especially when they live far away. And sometimes they're uncomfortable around the aged—"Do we have to go to Grandma's? It smells funny there."

Open my children's hearts, Lord. Help my children realize that their youth and vitality can really make an older relative's day. And use our parents to bless our children with their stories, wisdom, and unconditional affection.

Finally Lord, help our whole extended family to show the same kind of loyalty to each other that Ruth and Naomi shared. Show us one practical thing to do this week to make Grandma and Grandpa feel special. By Your grace, use us—from the oldest to the youngest—to carry out Your spiritual plan of redemption in our family.

Amen.

Confidence Builders

*We should go up and take possession of the land, for we can
certainly do it!*

Dear Lord,

How much I want each of my children to have the winning confidence
of Caleb who, against majority opinion, encouraged Israel to claim the
Promised Land. By the promises of Your Word and the power of Your
Spirit, I claim these confidence builders for my children today:

When they are tempted to doubt whether a life spent following
God is really worth the cost, may they hear You say, "Do not throw
away your confidence; if you persevere, I will richly reward you"
(from Heb. 10:35).

When they're anxious or discouraged, may they hear You say, "I am
the God of hope. Let me fill you with joy and peace so that you may
overflow with the power of the Holy Spirit" (from Rom. 15:13).

When they can't seem to break the pattern of negative thinking,
may they hear You say, "You can do anything and everything through
me. I will give you strength" (from Phil. 4:13).

When they feel trapped by habits or circumstances, may they hear
You say, "Where my Spirit is, you will find freedom" (from 2 Cor.
3:17).

When results seem a long time coming, may they hear You say,
"I am your provider; put your hope in me and wait for me" (from
Lam. 3:24).

When anguished prayers seem unanswered, may they hear You say,

"You have this assurance when you approach me: if you ask anything according to my will, I will hear you and answer you" (from 1 John 5:14-15).

When physical or emotional weakness slows them down, may they hear You say, "If you worship by my Spirit and glory in my Son, Christ Jesus, you never need to put your confidence for success in your own strength. I am able to make all grace abound to you, so that in all things at all times, having all that you need, you will excel in every good work" (from Phil. 3:3, 2 Cor. 9:8).

When every outward circumstance seems to go against them, may they hear You say, "Do not lose heart. Fix your eyes not on what you can see, but on what is unseen. For what you can see is temporary, but what is unseen is eternal" (from 2 Cor. 4:16,18).

When their skills and abilities seem insufficient for the task at hand, may they hear You say, "You don't need to be competent on your on own. Ultimately your competence comes from Me" (from 2 Cor. 3:4-5).

Lord, thank You that I can be totally confident that You hear my prayer today.

Amen.

If You Can't Say Something Nice . . .

Who is the man who desires life, and loves length of days that he may see good? Keep your tongue from evil, and your lips from speaking deceit.

PSALM 34:12-13, NASB

Lord,

I know You have ordained praise from the lips of children (Ps. 8:2). But sometimes children say things I know You didn't ordain at all.

And that's true about me, too. Help me today to have a gracious attitude in all that I say—especially to my children. The tongue is indeed a small part of our bodies, Lord, but oh, how much trouble it can get us into when we don't learn to master it (James 3:2-3,5).

I pray that my children will learn to watch their words. Help them not to say things they know aren't right (Ps. 34:12-13). Especially help them not to speak badly about others, quarrel with friends, or pick fights with their siblings (Titus 3:2).

Make my children increasingly conscious of how much power the tongue has to do good to others (James 3:9). May they use this power to be truly courteous and kind to all (Titus 3:2).

And in our family today, if we can't say something nice, Lord, help us to say nothing at all!

Amen.

Praise Inexpressible!

Though you have not seen him, you love him; and even though you do not see him now, you believe in him and are filled with an inexpressible and glorious joy.

1 PETER 1:8

PRAYING FROM 1 PETER 1:3-9

O God of my family,
I pray with Peter today. I take his holy outburst of joy as my own:

Praise to You, God and Father of our Lord Jesus Christ! In Your great mercy You have given my children hope—*real* hope—because they have new life in You (v. 3). All praise to You!

Praise to You, O God, for making this hope possible for my children through Jesus' resurrection from the dead. Yes, Jesus is Lord of our family! Jesus is the one who has given us an inheritance like no other. Unlike all other wealth my children could inherit, their incredible spiritual riches in Him can never spoil, fade, or be destroyed, because the riches are kept safe in heaven (v. 4). I exalt You, Lord!

Praise to You, God and Father of my children! By Your power, You promise to shield each one of them from danger through their faith in You. Your gift of salvation will always be at work in them—from the moment of forgiveness, through every challenge of life, to the very moment You return (v. 5). I worship You, wonderful Lord!

All praise to You, God! Even in the middle of trials and heartaches, my children can experience a joy that comes straight from heaven. Thank You that their troubles are only meant to prove, refine, and polish their faith so that it will shine like gold. Then when they stand before You, all praise, glory, and honor will belong to Jesus our Lord (vv. 6-7).

Yes, all praise to You, my God, for the gift of Jesus! Even though we've never seen Him as Peter did, we love Him. We believe in Him. My children and I treasure the prize of new life we are receiving through Him *right now*. And that's why we feel exactly what Peter felt—"inexpressible and glorious joy" (v. 8).

O God our Father, receive this family's grateful praise today. Amen.

Without Prejudice

If you show special attention to the man wearing fine clothes and say,
"Here's a good seat for you," but say to the poor man, "You stand there"
or "Sit on the floor by my feet," have you not discriminated among
yourselves and become judges with evil thoughts?

JAMES 2:3-4

Lord,

I thank You that You do not show favoritism or prejudice toward the
people You have created. Thank You that any human being can be
clothed with Christ despite his or her religious background, social sta-
tus, gender, race, or color (Gal. 3:27-28). May my children grow up
understanding that in You we are all one—and You are over all and in
all (Col. 3:11).

Today I pray that You will help my children not to hold unfair
opinions or reactions based on such things as money, clothes, or position (1 Tim. 5:21). Many kids are made fun of or rejected because of
something as silly as not having brand-name athletic shoes! May my
children treat a poorly dressed friend at school the same as a well-
dressed one (James 2:2-4)!

Father, please help me make our home a place where we do what is
right by loving our neighbor as ourselves—and without partiality
(James 2:8). And may my children be shining examples of a willingness
to go against the crowd, not only accepting those who are different but
embracing them.

Amen.

When a Parent's Soul Is Pierced

Then Simeon blessed them and said to Mary, his mother: "This child is destined to cause the falling and rising of many in Israel, and to be a sign that will be spoken against, so that the thoughts of many hearts will be revealed. And a sword will pierce your own soul too."

LUKE 2:34-35

Lord,

Today I pray that You would help me understand more about suffering and pain. I know You have come to bind up the brokenhearted (Isa. 61:1), and yet You allow us to experience all kinds of hurt here on earth.

In my parent heart I can imagine how painful it must have been for Mary to learn that her baby Jesus' destiny would pierce her very soul. How hard it is for any mother or father to watch a child suffer!

Help me to accept that my children will experience pain because we live in a sinful world—or even simply because they love You (John 15:20-21). Forgive me, Lord, when I want to protect my children so much that I would almost risk their destiny or calling to protect them from harm. Grant me the great courage of Mary. And give me the willingness not only to put Your will first but also to teach my children to say with Jesus, "Not my will, but thine, be done" (Luke 22:42, KJV).

Thank You that though pain and sorrow come in this life, nothing can rob us or our children of Your love or of eternal life with You (Rom. 8:38-39).

Amen.

Which Son Obeyed?

What do you think? There was a man who had two sons. He went to the first and said, "Son, go and work today in the vineyard."

"I will not," he answered, but later he changed his mind and went.

Then the father went to the other son and said the same thing. He answered, "I will, sir," but he did not go.

Which of the two did what his father wanted?

MATTHEW 21:28-31

Heavenly Father,

When I read this parable, I recognize my children. So often they say they'll do something—clean their room, complete homework, or finish a chore—but when I check to see what they've done, they haven't even begun!

Yet how quickly I also recognize myself. How easy it is for me to say, "Yes! Yes, Lord!" with gusto . . . only to walk away and do nothing. But Your Word teaches that if we love You, we *will* obey You (1 John 5:2) and that even Jesus learned obedience (Heb. 5:8). How serious this subject is then!

I know that I love You, Lord. And so do my children. I repent on behalf of my family for things left unsaid and undone, for promptings from You gone unheeded. Please help us replace easy affections with passionate obedience.

Thank You for the extraordinary blessings that will come to my children when they act on Your will (Deut. 28:1-14). Show each person in our house one meaningful step of obedience to take today.

Amen.

Indispensable Prayers

e sin against the Lord when we stop praying for others. When once we begin to see how absolutely indispensable intercession is, just as much a duty as loving God or believing in Christ, and how we are called and bound to it as believers, we shall feel that to cease intercession is grievous sin.

Let us ask for grace to take up our place as priests with joy, and give our life to bring down the blessing of heaven.

ANDREW MURRAY

Ask, Seek, Knock

Ask and it will be given to you; seek and you will find; knock and the door will be opened to you. For everyone who asks receives; he who seeks finds; and to him who knocks, the door will be opened.

MATTHEW 7:7-8

Heavenly Father,

How wonderful that You have invited us to seek You out, to knock on Your door, and to come in and make requests! I praise You, God. Thank You that You aren't like a busy dad who says, "Don't knock on my door. Don't ask for things. I'm too busy to be bothered!"

Today I pray that my kids will begin to comprehend how much their heavenly Father *wants* to be generous with them (Matt. 7:11). Your Word says we would receive more from You if we just asked for it (James 4:2). Help my kids to ask for the world! By my example and the Spirit's teaching, may they grow up learning to bring every need and desire—both great and small—to You. And may they learn to wrap each request in thankfulness and praise (Phil. 4:6).

Help my children to seek You while they're still young (Ps. 63:1, Jer. 29:13). May they be convinced throughout their lives that You *want* them to seek You—not because You're hiding but because You want to be found. Unlike me, You're never too busy, never unavailable. You never even sleep or nap (Ps. 121:3-4).

Thank You that Your door is always open and that You actually invite my children to pester You (Luke 18:1-7)! Teach us all how to ask, how to seek, and how to knock with confidence.

Amen.

Names That Shine

In the night I remember your name, O LORD.

PSALM 119:55

O Lord,

In the quiet of this house, in the shadows of fears, in the darkness of my limited ability to understand the present or see the future, I remember Your name. Your lovely names, my God, surround my sleeping children like lighted candles:

Friend of children. You will patiently call them to You, seek out their fellowship, and reward their simple trust (Matt. 19:13-14).

Redeemer. You have bought my children back from the penalty of sin and brought us into the family of God. You—only You—can create new beginnings over and over again in their lives (Rom. 6:23).

Wonderful Counselor. You will lead each child through tough choices (Isa. 42:16-17). You will make Your wisdom available without reproach when they ask (James 1:5).

Provider. You are the source of every good and perfect gift (James 1:17), of every bite of daily bread (Ps. 34:10).

Healer. You will bring healing to my children when they are sick or wounded in body, spirit, or emotion (Exod. 15:26, Jer. 17:14). You will renew my children day by day (Job 33:4).

None of Your many names can contain the awesome reality of You, but each one shines so brightly in this darkness!

Your name, O Lord, is worthy of our worship (Phil. 2:10). The earth is filled with Your love (Ps. 119:64), and so is this house. You fill our hearts with a great peace. And we can sleep secure.

Amen.

"Seven Times a Day I Praise You!"

The devotional writer of Psalm 119 tried to keep an awareness of God's goodness in mind at all times. In verse 164 he declared, "Seven times a day I praise you." Try these "praise minders" for a thankful family:

1. Getting up—praise for new beginnings and another day of life. "This is the day the LORD has made; let us rejoice and be glad in it" (Ps. 118:24).

2. Breakfast—praise for daily provisions. "You open your hand and satisfy the desires of every living thing" (Ps. 145:16).

3. Starting school or work—praise for meaningful tasks you can put your whole

hearts into. "That everyone may eat and drink, and find satisfaction in all his toil— this is the gift of God" (Eccles. 3:13).

4. Lunch—praise for health and strength. "The God of Israel gives power and strength to his people" (Ps. 68:35).

5. Transition hour before dinner. Praise for your limitations. "But he said to me, 'My grace is sufficient for you, for my power is made perfect in weakness'" (2 Cor. 12:9).

6. Dinner—praise for children. "Sons [and daughters] are a heritage from the LORD, children a reward from him" (Ps. 127:3).

7. Bedtime—praise for comfort and rest. "My people will live in peaceful dwelling places, in secure homes, in undisturbed places of rest" (Isa. 32:18).

When I Run from Prayer

B e merciful to me, my God. When I flee from prayer, it's not that I want to flee from You, but from myself and my own superficiality. I don't want to run away from Your Infinity and Holiness, but from the deserted marketplace of my own soul.

KARL RAHNER

The Upside-Down Kingdom

If anyone wants to be first, he must be the very last, and the servant of all.

MARK 9:35

Dear Lord,

Sometimes it's a challenge to teach my children about You because You ask us to do the opposite of what comes naturally. When we want to hate, You say love. When we want to run, You say stay. When we want to take, You say give.

Open my children's eyes today to the life-giving truths of Your upside-down kingdom:

If anyone wants to be first . . . Motivate my children to serve others, get last in line, and discover the joy of giving away the biggest piece. Help them check their urge to yell, "It's not fair!" at every opportunity.

Whoever loses his life for me and for the gospel will save it (Mark 8:35). The appeal of self-centeredness in our world is so strong. Show my children the greater attraction of being in right relationship with You and of receiving the eternal, abundant life You offer.

Love your enemies and pray for those who persecute you (Matt. 5:44). Help my children to see the hurt, fear, or need that so often explains the meanness of others. Prompt my children to pray for kids who treat them badly—and to experience the amazing peace that this radical response can bring.

By Your Spirit powerfully at work in my children, make them walking, talking demonstrations of the truth of Your upside-down gospel.

In Your name I pray. Amen.

The Restorer

Those from among you will rebuild the ancient ruins; you will raise up the age-old foundations; and you will be called the repairer of the breach, the restorer of the streets in which to dwell.

ISAIAH 58:12, NASB

Lord,

I want to start on a solid foundation to invite Your blessings into my children's lives. But my foundation has breaches and cracks from my past that need Your restoration work.

At times I find myself parenting in ways rooted in negative experiences. I repeat unhealthy patterns and behaviors from my childhood that I don't want myself or my children to embrace.

Show me a new way, Lord. I know that the shortcomings and sins of parents are handed down from generation to generation (Ezek. 18:19-20). But I also know that bondage can be broken as I face and forgive the past. Today please begin to break any of those chains that remain, and bring me the healing I need, Lord (Isa. 42:7, Jer. 17:14).

I know this is a process. So I ask You to reveal to me the areas where I need to forgive or to make different, healthier choices for my children. You are able to use for good even those years in my past that were sometimes painful (Joel 2:25). Thank You for Your powerful encouragement: "Forget the former things; do not dwell on the past. See, I am doing a new thing!" (Isa. 43:18-19).

Thank You that with Your help I can learn from my past instead of letting it hinder my future and my children's future. I praise You for this today, my Restorer and Redeemer.

Amen.

The Promises of God

he promises of God

Will surely come to pass.

I'll stand upon His Word

And trust and see

How faithful He will be

Who died for me.

For He exalted His Word

Above all His Name.

The promises of God

Will surely come to pass.

ROY HICKS JR.

The Narrow Way

Make every effort to enter through the narrow door, because many, I tell you, will try to enter and will not be able to. . . . Small is the gate and narrow the road that leads to life, and only a few find it.

LUKE 13:24, MATTHEW 7:14

Lord,

Sometimes this world feels like a twelve-lane, one-way freeway crammed with traffic rushing toward the horizon. High speed, high-tech, mega bass, tinted windows rolled up—everybody trying to get there first and in the finest style.

There *where?*

Save us, Jesus, from the worldly freeway that's going nowhere. Put us on the narrow path that leads to You and to life.

You have said that many will miss the gate to eternal life. This could frighten me if I thought it was up to my children to find the way alone. Thank You, loving Lord, that if they truly seek You, You will show my children the path to life (Isa. 42:16).

Help me teach them today that "everybody's doing it" is a weak (and boring) reason to do something—that high ratings, big money, beautiful appearance, and front-page news have little to do with whether something is worthy. Or life-giving. Or of the Spirit.

I pray that my children will be among the few who "make every effort" today. Show them where to turn and what to leave behind. Help them hear Your voice saying, "This is the way . . ." (Isa. 30:21) each day until they step through the narrow door into eternity.

Amen.

Shaped by Him

Don't let the world around you squeeze you into its own mold, but let
God re-mold your minds from within, so that you may prove in practice
that the plan of God for you is good, meets all his demands and moves
toward the goal of true maturity.

ROMANS 12:2, PH

Merciful Lord,

You have shown Your grace to me and my family. I seek Your will today
for me and the ones I love. You are a God of unfailing kindness
(Isa. 54:8), and I thank You!

Lord Jesus, draw _____ to You today. Pursue my child, as You
did Paul. As You have me.

My child is Your workmanship, created in Jesus to fulfill Your perfect will (Eph. 2:10). Shape _____ in mind, body, spirit, and heart
to please and serve You. Don't let the world shape the one I—and
You—love so dearly (Rom. 12:1-2).

Lord, Your will for my child is good (Jer. 29:11). Help him experience Your goodness today, to see through the world's deceptions. Al-
though they promise good, they deliver trouble (Prov. 10:22). But every
good thing comes from You (James 1:17).

Renew my child's life today, You who make all things new
(Ps. 119:156, 2 Cor. 5:17). Lead my child into Your pleasing and perfect will for the days ahead (Rom. 12:2).

We are Yours, all Yours (John 17:9)! Keep on changing all of us
into Your beautiful likeness (2 Cor. 3:18).

In Your great name I pray. Amen.

The Treasures of Wisdom

My son, if your heart is wise, then my heart will be glad; my inmost being will rejoice when your lips speak what is right.

PROVERBS 23:15

Dear Lord,

I plead for my children that they will grow every day in wisdom and good reputation as You did (Luke 2:52). Help me do my part to raise them to be wise adults, able to make right choices that will bring each one a lifetime of blessing—and bring You glory!

May they know, first of all, that to hold You in awe is the beginning of all wisdom (Ps. 111:10); You are the source of the kind of knowledge and understanding we need to build our lives on (Prov. 2:6). Your truth brings us victory (2:7), safety (2:8), protection from evil people (2:11), living at ease without fear (1:33), a wealth more precious than gold (3:13-14), and material wealth, too (3:9-10)!

Yes, Lord, You hold each of these in store for my children if they commit themselves to a lifelong search for the treasures of wisdom (2:1-4).

Teach my children early that some things this world values as smart and essential are actually foolishness in Your sight (1 Cor. 3:19). Pride, envy, selfish ambition—these are not the wisdom from above (James 3:13-16). Neither are such "all-American virtues" as self-reliance (Prov. 3:5), speaking our minds (17:28), keeping score (19:11), and making sure we get the credit we deserve (27:2).

May my children grow up wise only as You define wisdom! Lord, only by Your Spirit and the truth of Your Word can my children's minds be renewed with the wisdom that comes from heaven. Grant them Your sweet, life-giving treasures: purity, consideration, humility, mercy, fairness, and sincerity (James 3:17).

May character strengths like these be a light to their paths (Prov. 6:23) and a garland of grace on their heads (Prov. 4:9), as You've promised. And may my children never see as foolish the crucified Christ. The cross—offensive and weak as it seems to so many—You have made the symbol of Your ultimate power and wisdom (1 Cor. 1:23-24). May my children always remember that knowing You personally is the best human knowledge of all.

Amen.

What Is Better

"Martha, Martha," the Lord answered, "you are worried and upset about many things, but only one thing is needed. Mary has chosen what is better, and it will not be taken away from her."

LUKE 10:41

Lord and Savior,

Like Martha, I get so busy and distracted sometimes. It's easy to forget about the things that matter most: worshiping You, listening to You, being in Your presence.

Lord, I want to teach my children to renew their strength by spending time at Your feet. These days even kids get too busy! As they get caught up in their own hectic schedules, help them to sort out what is truly important. Remind them to take time just to sit before You and be with You. In Your presence—even for a few minutes each day—they can find rest and peace (Jer. 6:16).

As they grow up, I pray my children will learn not just how to *do* but how to *be*. Not just how to stay *busy* but how to stay *still*. And within that stillness to hear Your quiet voice:

You, dear child, are from God and will overcome, because the one who is in you is greater than the one who is in the world (from 1 John 4:4).

Amen.

A Humble Inheritance

The meek and lowly are fortunate! for the whole wide world belongs to them.

MATTHEW 5:5, TLB

Heavenly Father,

How much I long for my children to have confidence, to excel, to believe in their own abilities and strengths. And yet, I also know how dangerous the wrong kind of pride can be.

Help my children understand that a humble spirit will be blessed and guided by You (Ps. 25:9). Show them the difference between thinking too much of themselves and seeing themselves accurately (Rom. 12:3). Teach them to love the praise of God more than the praise of men (John 12:43).

I know if my children are haughty rather than humble, they will run into all kinds of trouble (Prov. 16:18). Help my children understand that if they are humble, You will be the one who lifts them up (James 4:10), who helps them triumph—at school, in sports, in life.

What gifts do my children have that You did not give them? I thank You for all of their accomplishments, and I pray that through them, Father of Light, You will shine brightly (James 1:17).

Amen.

Equal Favor

The boys grew up, and Esau became a skillful hunter, a man of the open country, while Jacob was a quiet man, staying among the tents. Isaac, who had a taste for wild game, loved Esau, but Rebekah loved Jacob.

GENESIS 25:27-28

Heavenly Father,

It is hard to understand how a parent could love one child and not the other, as Isaac and Rebekah appeared to do. And yet I know I show favoritism, usually without even realizing it (James 2:9)!

Today I pray that You would show both parents in this house how we can be like-minded, sharing the same love and purpose for our kids (Phil. 2:2). When one child seems to enjoy our interests more than another or is taking more of our time, show us how to be sensitive to the other children so they don't feel overlooked or neglected.

Above all, help us not to be divided as parents, even though we sometimes have differing ideas about what one of our kids needs or about how to discipline and love him well. Help us work together as a team, as crucial parts of the same body—our family—each being the parent God desires (1 Cor. 12:15-18).

Show us as parents how to validate our children's unique qualities. Help our kids not to be rivals in unhealthy ways but instead to encourage and build each other up (1 Thess. 5:11). May they never need to compete for our love, because they're confident in our equal favor and affection every day.

Amen.

The Most High

He who dwells in the shelter of the Most High will rest in the shadow of the Almighty.

PSALM 91:1

PRAYING PSALM 91

Almighty God, Most High,
Yes, I often forget that You are Lord, God above all gods. Today, I will lay all my concerns for _____ before You, but *I will not forget who You are*: the Most High, the Almighty One (v. 1)!

That's why I can pray now with confident hope.

Because of who You are, deliver my child from fears, from harm at night, from snares of all kinds, from injury and illness (vv. 3-6).

Because of who You are, command Your angels to guard my child, to lift her up, and carry her past many troubles. (vv. 11-12).

You, Lord, are her true home and eternal refuge. Yes, You will rescue my child. You have promised to protect, save, and honor us if we acknowledge who You really are—and trust You completely (vv. 14-15).

In Jesus' name. Amen.

An Exciting Secret

And this is the secret: Christ in your hearts is your only hope of glory.

COLOSSIANS 1:27, TLB

PRAYING FROM COLOSSIANS

Dear Heavenly Father,

May the life of Christ beam forth from my kids' faces today like an exciting secret they can't quite contain! Jesus Christ in us *is* God's secret to life—and to our family's joy (1:27; 3:4). Apart from Christ's presence and power, we are such an ordinary family.

But You, Father, have made us alive and new in Christ (2:13). Now when You look at each peanut-butter-smudged child or harried parent in this house, You see the shining beauty of Christ (3:3)!

Today, may that beauty continue to work in my child and continue to change her—inside and out. May the peace of Christ replace every fearful thought, every insecurity and worry. May Christ's peace surround my child like a divine hug all day long (3:15).

And whatever happens today, may my child do everything with a heart full of joy in the name of Christ—every word, every thought, every action (3:17).

Yes, this is my sincere prayer for each child: Christ in _____! Christ in _____! Christ in _____! And always, Christ in me!

In His precious name I pray. Amen.

Thy Answers Make Me . . .

y prayers, my God,

flow from what I am not;

I think thy answers

make me what I am.

GEORGE MACDONALD

Have Mercy on Them

The sacrifices of God are a broken spirit; a broken and contrite heart,
O God, you will not despise.

PSALM 51:17

PRAYING FROM PSALM 51

Heavenly Father,
Today I pray David's prayer of confession on behalf of my children.
Ezra repented sincerely on behalf of his people (Ezra 9), and Jesus cried
out from the cross, "Forgive them, for they do not know what they are
doing" (Luke 23:34). In this same way, I plead for Your forgiveness for
those who can't always ask for it themselves.

Have mercy on my children! Because You are a compassionate
God, I'm asking You to completely blot out all their sins, little and large
(v. 1). I see my children's misdeeds and selfish natures close up every
day—they're so much like me, Lord! (v. 3). And in my own frustration
about their disobedience, sometimes I forget that it matters so much
more that they're also disobeying You (v. 4).

You see each heart in this house completely, and all Your judgments
are true and fair. As human beings, my children have been capable of
going their own way since before they were born (v. 5).

Yet Your loving desire is for my children to be true and good in the
deepest corners of their hearts. I can't make this happen, but You are
able to touch places in their souls that I can't reach. You can teach my
children wisdom, integrity, and purity in their deepest natures (v. 6).

Only You, Lord, can truly cleanse my children and make them

white as snow (v. 7). Wash my kids today, and they will be truly clean—and able to sing with joy again (v. 8). Thank You for being willing to look away from my children's sins (v. 9). Create a clean heart in them, Lord. Give them a fresh start so they will have a sweet and sincerely obedient spirit (v. 10).

Please don't ever give up on them or leave them (v. 11). I plead with You to show them how much happiness they can find in loving and obeying Your ways in the days ahead.

In Jesus' precious name. Amen.

Willing Workers

Whatever you do, work at it with all your heart, as working for the Lord, not for men.

COLOSSIANS 3:23

Lord of the Harvest,

Our home always seems to be in need of workers, but so often the help-ing hands are few. It takes all of us working together to keep our home running well. Help me to teach my children to be willing workers, earning the respect of others (1 Thess. 4:12), especially their parents.

Your Word says that lazy hands will make a man poor, but diligent hands bring wealth (Prov.10:4). May my children learn while they are young how to reach for a task with enthusiasm—and without com-plaining (Phil. 2:14).

In fact, show my children how to do chores as if they were actually doing them for You—not just because they have to (Col. 3:23).

Help each of us, Father, to do our part so that we will all be joined in Christ and share one goal (Eph. 4:16): a happy, clean home!

Amen.

A Good Reputation

A good name is more desirable than great riches; to be esteemed is better than silver or gold.

PROVERBS 22:1

Jesus, Faithful Shepherd,

Thank You that You know each of us so well You call us by name (John 10:3). Today I lift the names of my children to You, and I praise You for each little lamb You've given me.

You have said that a good name is worth more to my children than great riches (Prov. 22:1). Please help my children value a good reputation. Let love and faithfulness be so much a part of my children's lives that they win favor not only from You but from their peers, teachers, family, and all who know them or hear of them (Luke 2:52).

Most of all, I pray that their character would bring praise to You, Lord. May Your light shine so brightly in them that it will be obvious to everyone that they love You, and people will have no choice but to praise You and give You all the credit for their goodness (Matt. 5:16).

Amen.

Ten Tips for Praying Attentively

Choose times, places, and postures that work best for you. (Standing by a window three times a day worked for Daniel.)

2. Harness the prayer energy that comes from deeply felt needs of the moment. (Finding himself in the fish's belly worked wonders for Jonah's prayer life.)

3. Pray from notes; keep a quiet-time notebook.

4. Keep referring to a written collection of "prayer principles" (for example, "God lives with the contrite and lowly spirit," from Isa. 57:15) that you feel especially prone to forget.

5. Pray with photographs of your children in front of you.

6. Pray briefly about the topic that distracted you.

7. When something from your to-do list comes to mind, jot it down, then return quickly to prayer.

8. Pray aloud or in a whisper, especially if you're sleepy.

9. Be firm with yourself about mental wanderings, but don't scold. God isn't shocked at your humanity.

10. Ask God to strengthen your concentration powers for prayer. He cares about your relationship with Him more than you do.

WARREN AND RUTH MYERS

Slips and Spills

You hem me in—behind and before; you have laid your hand upon me.

PSALM 139:5

Heavenly Father,

Today I pray that You will protect my children from little and big accidents in every way. Hem them in—no matter where they are.

You know my kids, Lord—they think they're invincible. Especially _____. He has no fear of falling from trees or slipping off skateboards. Sometimes I'm afraid to let him loose for a minute!

Lord, in the face of my child's blindness to danger, I confess that sometimes that's all I see. I'm so glad that You see everything. And You are everywhere, like the wind rustling the trees outside my window. You aren't limited by time, distractions, or only one set of eyes. There's no place my kids can go where they are outside of Your care (Ps. 139:7).

Give me Your spirit of peace today, Heavenly Father. I don't want fear and my active imagination to prevent me from enjoying my children's little risks and grand accomplishments. Today I put my trust—not only in helmets and kneepads—but in You.

Please strengthen my faith as I learn to celebrate my children's natural love of life.

Amen.

That One Thing

One thing I do: . . . I press on toward the goal to win the prize.

PHILIPPIANS 3:13-14

Dear Lord Jesus,

Today I ask that You will help my children choose the few important things—those "one things" in Your Word—that really matter.

May my children *know* one thing above all—that You are the source of salvation. Give them the assurance of the man Jesus healed who said, "One thing I do know. I was blind but now I see!" (John 9:25).

Lead my children to *experience* one thing above all—that Your love for them is true and unfailing. When trials come, may they be able to testify with Jeremiah: "This [one thing] I call to mind and therefore I have hope: Because of the LORD's great love we are not consumed, for his compassions never fail. They are new every morning" (Lam. 3:21-23).

May my children *desire* one thing above all—to spend time in Your presence worshiping You. With David, may they love to sing: "One thing I ask of the LORD, this is what I seek: that I may dwell in the house of the LORD all the days of my life, to gaze upon the beauty of the LORD and to seek him in his temple" (Ps. 27:4).

And with Paul, may my children *strive* for one thing above all—to lead a life that wins Your approval. "One thing I do: Forgetting what is behind and straining toward what is ahead, I press on toward the goal to win the prize for which God has called me heavenward in Christ Jesus" (Phil. 3:13-14).

With single-hearted devotion, may my children please You in all things.

In Jesus' name I pray. Amen.

Asking with Earnestness

Supplication means to ask with earnestness, with intensity, with perseverance. It is a declaration that we are deadly serious about this prayer business. We are going to keep at it and not give up. John Calvin wrote, "We must repeat the same supplications not twice or three times only, but as often as we have need, a hundred and a thousand times. . . . We must never be weary in waiting for God's help."

RICHARD FOSTER

This Grace of Giving

But just as you excel in everything—in faith, in speech, in knowledge, in complete earnestness and in your love for us—see that you also excel in this grace of giving.

2 CORINTHIANS 8:7

Heavenly Father,
You withhold no good thing from us (Ps. 84:11). Today I pray that You would help my children learn that it is more blessed to give than to receive (Acts 20:35).

May giving be a lifestyle in our home—not just something we think about on special holidays or at a birthday party but anytime we see someone in need (Matt. 5:42).

Sometimes it is harder for my children to share what is familiar—their own bike or a special book—than it is to give a store-bought gift. Show my children that the greatest gifts are often those that personally cost them something to give (2 Cor. 8:2).

And finally, help my children to give and to share with pure motives—happily, freely, but not to show off their generosity or to expect a return (2 Cor. 9:7).

Amen.

Children of God

The Spirit himself testifies with our spirit that we are God's children.

ROMANS 8:16

MEDITATIONS TO CARRY THROUGH THE DAY

Heavenly Father,
How grateful I am to be Your child! And how glad I am to know that my children are first of all Your children. May my kids know this deep in their souls. And may they become convinced that You love them even more than I possibly can.

Today, I meditate on Your promises:

How great is the love the Father has lavished on _____, that he or
she should be called a child of God! And that is what he or she is!
(1 John 3:1)

As a mother comforts her child,
so you, Lord, will comfort _____.
(Isa. 66:13)

Yet to all who receive him, including _____,
to those who believe in his name,
he gives the right to become children of God.
(John 1:12)

Those who are led by the Spirit of God are sons of God.
(Rom. 8:14)

Clean All Through

Live no longer as the unsaved do, for they are blinded and confused.
Their closed hearts are full of darkness; they are far away from the life of
God because they have shut their minds against him. . . . They don't
care anymore about right and wrong.

EPHESIANS 4:17-19, TLB

Holy Lord,

Paul's warnings almost perfectly describe the numbness that passes for "cul-
ture" or "being hip" today. Please save my children from this terrible decep-
tion! Help them to "hold on to faith and a good conscience" (1 Tim. 1:19).

Release Your Word and Your Spirit in our family to keep us spiritually sensitive. Instead of competing to be contemporary or accepted—in
TV, movie, or music choices; in our attitudes about sex; or in how we
treat others—may our family members spur each other on toward love
and good deeds (Heb. 10:24).

Show me, Lord, how to nourish a home that champions a good conscience. When one of my children needs direction or correction, help me
not to react with casual indifference or overreact with shaming anger.
Whether the offense is a stolen cookie, a lie, or a sexual compromise—go
before me as I try to lead my child back to repentance and a new start.

Thank You that we can always draw near to You in full assurance of
faith, knowing that our hearts have been cleansed from a guilty conscience by the blood of Christ (Heb. 10:22).

And may the meditations of our hearts always be pleasing in Your
sight, O Lord, our wonderful redeemer (Ps. 19:14).

Amen.

Holy Fingerprints

The earth is filled with your love, O LORD.

PSALM 119:64

Creator Lord,

As my children grow up, I pray that like the psalmists, they will find Your fingerprints all over the world. May they see Your handiwork in every corner of ordinary life and praise You!

May they notice Your touch in the nature that surrounds them each day as they walk to school. And when they peek at the stars before going to bed, may they sense Your awesome power. For "the heavens declare the glory of God; the skies proclaim the work of his hands" (Ps. 19:1).

May my children think of You when they hear beautiful music. Remind them that You are the one who blessed us with music and the ability to feel it deep in our souls. "It is good to praise the LORD and make music to your name, O Most High, to proclaim your love in the morning and your faithfulness at night" (Ps. 92:1).

May my children see You in the beauty of different faces and races from all over the earth. And may they see Your creative wonders even in their friends and siblings. "Did not he who made me in the womb make them? . . . Come, let us bow down in worship, let us kneel before the LORD, our Maker" (Job 31:15; Ps. 95:6).

Thank You, Lord, that everywhere my children look, they will find evidence today that You are here.

Amen.

Heavy-Handed

Fathers, don't over-correct your children, or you will take all the heart out of them.

COLOSSIANS 3:21, PH

A FATHER'S PRAYER

Heavenly Father,

Today I feel clunky, clumsy, and not very efficient—like a truck tire out of balance. I say things I shouldn't (usually at high volume), and don't say things I should. When I try to bend something, it just breaks. Please help me, Father of fathers, not to take the heart out of my kids!

Tie down my tongue when something shouldn't be said or when You know I'll say it all wrong. Turn my words from bullying to encouraging. Help me to listen long instead of trying to fix things fast.

Show me how to make a point without yelling, to restrain without squashing. Erase from my mind, at least for a while, all the sentences that begin "Kids these days . . ." and "When I was a boy . . ."

Hear my prayer, Abba, Father. Every day I want to walk into my house with a blameless heart (Ps. 101:2). I want to be quick to say, "I do this because of what the LORD did for me" (Exod. 13:8). I want to be "above reproach"—managing my family well and raising children who obey me with respect and affection (1 Tim. 3:2-4).

By Your mercies, help me be merciful. By Your grace, give me graces. Because what I want to hear today is Your voice all through the house saying, "This is my much loved son in whom I am well pleased."

Amen.

A Blessing for Unity

ay the God who gives endurance and encouragement give you a spirit of unity among yourselves as you follow Christ Jesus, so that with one heart and mouth you may glorify the God and Father of our Lord Jesus Christ.

ROMANS 15:5-6

Raising Peacemakers

Let us therefore make every effort to do what leads to peace.

ROMANS 14:19

Prince of Peace,

Today I pray that my children might be peacemakers and sons of God
(Matt. 5:9). I pray that they would know Your peace that passes understanding (Phil. 4:7) and as a result that their peaceable love would overflow to others (1 Thess. 3:12).

Help my children to live in harmony—so far as it is possible for
them—with their parents, teachers, and peers (Heb. 12:14). May they
be devoted to their siblings in brotherly (and sisterly) love (Rom.
12:10). Help them to stop and think twice when they are tempted to
pay back one wrong with another (1 Thess. 5:15).

Lord, You Yourself declared, "Blessed are the peacemakers"
(Matt. 5:9). How heartily I agree with You! May my children be among
the first not only to avoid a quarrel but to help others do the same.

Show me how, day by day, to raise children to cherish unity and
harmony in Your kingdom.

In Jesus' name. Amen.

Advice from Heaven

Then Manoah prayed to the LORD: "O Lord, I beg you, let the man of God you sent to us come again to teach us how to bring up the boy who is to be born."

JUDGES 13:8

Heavenly Father,

I've never heard an angel talk to me about my kids, but I thank You that You have a special plan for each one of them. And like Manoah, I beg You to show me how to raise them according to Your wishes. Through Your Word and Your Holy Spirit, reveal to me what each of my children needs in order to grow up in Your favor.

Lord, maybe my children's destinies are something less unusual than Samson's delivering a nation from its enemies. But I thank You that they *do* have a special calling from You on their lives.

May I be as diligent in seeking Your wisdom as Samson's father was. When You do show me Your will, I pray that I will be faithful to follow all of Your instructions. And may my children strive through their own obedience to attain the great destiny You have waiting for them.

Finally, Lord, when I or my children foolishly get in the way of Your good purposes, I thank You that You will continue to accomplish Your wonderful purposes *in spite of us* all the days of our lives.

Amen.

A Mother Who Knows Best

*One day Naomi her mother-in-law said to her, "My daughter, should I
not try to find a home for you, where you will be well provided for? Is
not Boaz, with whose servant girls you have been, a kinsman of ours?
Tonight he will be winnowing barley on the threshing floor. Wash and
perfume yourself, and put on your best clothes. Then go down to the
threshing floor, but don't let him know you are there until he has
finished eating and drinking. When he lies down, note the place where
he is lying. Then go and uncover his feet and lie down. He will tell you
what to do."*

"I will do whatever you say," Ruth answered.

RUTH 3:1-5

A MOTHER'S PRAYER

Heavenly Father,

Today I pray that You would make me as wise as Naomi. She spoke
with confidence, and she was right about Boaz. She discerned what
Your plan might be for Ruth's life, and she cooperated with You in
bringing it about.

Naomi wasn't Ruth's own mother—yet she earned Ruth's trust
through years of faithful love in spite of suffering, loss, and hardship.
May I win my daughter's trust as well. May she see in me a faith so ap-
pealing that she will want to make it her own.

Father, so much has changed since Ruth's time—the customs, the
meanings, the way the sexes approach one another. But a daughter's
need for motherly guidance will never change. May You continue to

give me worthy insight, and may my daughter continue to seek my advice about friends, boys, dating—and even, as in Naomi's case, about what to wear!

Thank You, God, for the privilege of looking out for my daughter. Grant me wisdom to know Your best and the courage to reach for it. And grant my daughter a loyal and teachable heart like Ruth's.

Amen.

The Promise of Heaven

But our citizenship is in heaven.

PHILIPPIANS 3:20

Lord,

How I praise You and thank You for the promise of heaven! Sometimes I forget how temporary and fleeting this life on earth is.

Today my children and I will meditate on our future home and remind each other of the good news:

> In our Father's house there are many rooms.
> He is there now, preparing a place for our family;
> for _____, _____, and _____ .
> And He will come back and take us to be with Him.
> (John 14:2-4)

> When this earthly tent of our bodies is used up,
> we will live in a new building from God—
> an eternal house in heaven,
> not built by human hands.
> (2 Cor. 5:1)

Return of a Son

But while he was still a long way off, his father saw him and was filled with compassion for him.

Heavenly Father,

I pray today about that time in the future when one of my children may leave the house of Your favor and get lost in the dark. Lord, I don't want this ever to happen, yet I know that in small and large ways, I am a prodigal every day.

When my child wants to try out the pleasures life has to offer—and is willing to compromise his commitments to do so—have mercy on him. Thank You that if my son is faithless, You will remain faithful (2 Tim. 2:13). Be patient with him, Lord. I know You may need to bring him to a low point before You get his attention, before he can begin to see that what looked like a glittering landscape is really a pigpen.

During his times of wandering, doubting, rebelling, or just plain laziness, pursue him, Lord, and bring him back. He is the son of my heart—and of Yours as well! If the day comes when he can't remember *whose* he is, speak to him. I know You set apart Your chosen ones for Yourself (Ps. 4:3) and call each one by name (Isa. 43:1).

Lord, on that day of return, do Your redeeming miracle—turn those wasted years into assets You can greatly use. May Your tender discipline give him a sincere and lasting love for You and an even deeper regard for You as Lord (Ps. 119:67,71). Heal his waywardness completely, Lord, and love him freely (Hos. 14:4).

Amen.

Forgiven Much

Then [Jesus] turned toward the woman and said to Simon, "Do you see this woman? I came into your house. You did not give me any water for my feet, but she wet my feet with her tears and wiped them with her hair. You did not give me a kiss, but this woman, from the time I entered, has not stopped kissing my feet. You did not put oil on my head, but she has poured perfume on my feet. Therefore, I tell you, her many sins have been forgiven—for she loved much. But he who has been forgiven little loves little."

LUKE 7:44-47

Dear Jesus,

How this story encourages me! Every day I have so much to be forgiven for. Thank You for Your grace and mercy.

Parenting is hard for me. And growing up is hard for my kids, too. We fail daily; no one here is without sin (Isa. 64:6). Forgive us, Lord. Accept our sincere repentance and worship today.

I pray that each parent and each child in our house would be like the woman in this story—loving You devotedly, thankfully, and with his or her whole being. We want to perfume Your feet, Jesus, with our words, deeds, and attitudes. Show us how to love You extravagantly—to serve You and others in ways that really cost us something.

Thank You that You forgive our sins if we're faithful to confess them (1 John 1:9). Thank You that our confession changes Your memory—that You no longer recall our failures but only Your incredible love for us (Ps. 25:7).

In Your gracious name I pray. Amen.

Early Salvation

Remember your Creator in the days of your youth, before the days of trouble come.

ECCLESIASTES 12:1

Loving Heavenly Father,

Before dawn, I pray for my children. See each one asleep, Lord, zipped snugly into a flannel cocoon or swirling like a dancer in twisted sheets.

In so many ways they're still asleep in their childhood, yet I pray that at the youngest age possible they would seek You and respond to You (Ps. 63:1). I ask specifically this morning that my children will receive salvation early in their lives—before troubles and distractions and ambitions get in the way (Eccles. 12:1-8).

Early, Lord, because my children even at their sweetest and most innocent—yes, even from birth—need a Savior (Ps. 51:5).

Use the Scriptures planted in their hearts from infancy, as You did with Timothy, to draw them to You (2 Tim. 3:15). May Your Holy Spirit break through any spiritual barriers that are keeping them from asking to be born into Your kingdom (John 3:5-6).

Yes, early, Lord, because You invited children to know You and love You. And because You have promised that everyone—even someone who sleeps inside zippered flannel—can receive the power to become a child of God (John 1:12).

I ask this in Jesus' powerful name. Amen.

Welcome to Our Home

Offer hospitality to one another without grumbling.

1 PETER 4:9

Lord,

Today I pray that You would teach my children and me how to be good hosts. I want to be a good example to my children of Your gracious love.

Help me teach my children to be a real part of making our home cozy and welcoming so that both friends and strangers feel accepted (Heb. 13:2). May my children learn to consider what others might feel, to ask good questions, and to be sensitive to their friends' needs and put them first (Phil. 2:4).

Show my kids how much we have to share—whether it's a snack, a long sit on our couch, or an invitation to dinner (even if it's just leftovers).

How I thank You that You are a welcoming God! Someday You will make each of us feel at home at a great wedding feast (Rev. 19:7). Until that time, You promise to come in and make a home in our hearts (Rev. 3:20).

Amen.

Hard Love

This is the message you heard from the beginning: We should love one another.

1 JOHN 3:11

Lord,

Sometimes the hardest place to love is at home, and the hardest ones to express love to are the ones we love most. On days when irritations and grudges threaten to tear my children apart—from us their parents and from each other—may Your Spirit of love bring a healing presence.

By Your love working in them, help my children to love at all times (Prov. 17:17) and not just in words—"I *said* I was sorry!"—but with sincerity and with actions (1 John 3:18).

Help my children to be growing in:

—compassion (to try to understand the other person's experience),

—kindness (to show generosity and goodwill to others),

—humility (to remember their own shortcomings),

—gentleness (to respect each other's sensitivities),

—patience (to value what only time can accomplish [Col. 3:12]).

Show us how to love when it's hard, Lord. And teach us to forgive as You forgave us (Col. 3:13).

In Your name I pray. Amen.

Little Relinquishments

Give yourselves completely to God—every part of you—for you are back from death and you want to be tools in the hands of God, to be used for His good purposes.

ROMANS 6:13, TLB

Lord,

I want to give myself completely to You, but parts of me are so unattractive. Today I want especially to lay on Your altar those weak parts of my personality that I use as if they were strengths: my "mature reticence" to ask forgiveness from a toddler or a teenager; my nearly "faultless memory" of offenses suffered at the hands of others; my "blazing insight" in spotting a problem before a potential catastrophe; my slice-'n-dice logic in upbraiding and disheartening a struggling child when well-chosen words of praise would uplift and encourage.

And on Your altar, I also lay down those unappealing "strengths" of my children. They show up here every day, too.

Perhaps today we will have nothing beautiful or holy to give You, Lord. Please accept these unsightly offerings then. Help us to let them go like a pacifier left behind the couch because no one here uses it anymore. Receive these little relinquishments as humble gifts for our beautiful and holy Lord.

You have brought us back from death for something better, and we want to be tools in Your hands for Your good purposes today.

In Jesus' name. Amen.

Growth Rings

Let us leave the elementary teachings about Christ and go on to maturity.

HEBREWS 6:1

Dear Lord,

I pray today for maturity in my children. May each child live in a vital union with You—like an apple tree getting nutrients from the soil. May my children's roots go deep into Your Word. May their faith flourish over time, resulting in a full life that pleases You (Col. 2:6-7).

Show me how I can be part of nourishing my children toward emotional and spiritual maturity. May my example and every influence of this home help instead of hinder their growth.

Show us where our family is stuck in elementary thinking or childish behavior. Especially help _____ put to use what she has been taught so she can experience the benefit of right choices (Heb. 5:14).

Thank You that my children don't have to go through growth spurts alone. Through You, my children already have everything they need for spiritual and character growth (2 Pet. 1:3). In Your time, may each of my children show the "growth rings" described by Peter:

—adding good behavior to their declarations of faith;

—and to their good behavior, adding a real understanding of what You want;

—and to their understanding, adding the self-control and persistence necessary for mature living (2 Pet. 1:5-6).

Thank You that You came to earth so my children could have an abundant life and reach full maturity in You (John 10:10).

Amen.

A Harvest of Faith

Be rooted in him and founded upon him, continually strengthened by
the faith as you were taught it and your lives will overflow.

COLOSSIANS 2:7, PH

PRAYING THE PARABLE OF THE SOWER
(MATT. 13:1-23)

Lord of the Harvest,
Show me the parenting truths in this parable.

"A farmer went out to sow his seed. As he was scattering the seed, some fell along the path, and the birds came and ate it up" (vv. 3-4,19).

Lord, help my kids to understand and enthusiastically receive Your truths. May they listen carefully with both their minds and spirits when I teach them about Your kingdom. Keep Satan from snatching away my attempts.

"Some fell on rocky places, where it did not have much soil. It sprang up quickly. . . . But when the sun came up, the plants were scorched, and they withered because they had no root" (vv. 5-6,20-21).

Lord, it's so much easier for my kids to thrive spiritually during high points like Bible camp or pizza night at youth group. Help the commitments they make to You survive the hard times. Turn strong emotions into genuine character qualities that will be with them their whole lives.

"Other seed fell among thorns, which grew up and choked the plants" (vv. 7,22).

Lord, please help my children not to let their love for You get crowded out by competing desires, temptations, or affections. Prevent unconfessed sins or spiritual compromise from separating them from Your power. May they be diligent in weeding out anything that doesn't please You.

"Still other seed fell on good soil, where it produced a crop—a hundred, sixty or thirty times what was sown" (vv. 8,23).

Lord, show me how to tend the soil of my children's hearts. May they not only receive Your words but act on them and continue to grow spiritually throughout their lives. May my children lead many others to You, and may their lives bear a tremendous harvest of blessing.

Amen.

Persist and Prosper

Lazy people want much but get little, while the diligent are prospering.

PROVERBS 13:4, TLB

My Heavenly Father,

I stand in Your presence today on behalf of my children's work attitudes. Hear my prayers, Father. I'm not praying from a position of arrogance or self-righteousness or judgment.

Show me how to lead my child toward diligence—by example, by discipline, by encouragement. Today help me look for ways to teach:

—that laziness only leads to poverty and disgrace (Prov. 10:4-5),

—that lying around wishing for something never gets it for anyone (Prov. 28:19),

—that a person who is unwilling to work should not expect to live off the work of others (2 Thess. 3:10).

Deliver my children when they are tempted to laziness and carelessness. By Your power, cast out any evil spirits, influences, or bad habits that would bind them. Show me, Lord, if there is a deeper cause of laziness that should be addressed.

Father, so many contemporary heroes of kids really believe that good things should happen without effort. Deliver us from this lie of Satan—he is the great robber, the patron of slackers, the huckster of shortcuts, easy outs, and dead ends. But we belong to You, not him!

With praise and expectation I pray in Jesus' name. Amen.

A Blessing for God's Light

ay the light of God surround you today. May His light shine on your path for seeing, in your heart for peace, and from your face as a gift to others.

FROM PROVERBS 6:23

A Letter from Christ

You yourselves are our letter, written on our hearts, known and read by everybody. You show that you are a letter from Christ, the result of our ministry, written not with ink but with the Spirit of the living God, not on tablets of stone but on tablets of human hearts.

2 CORINTHIANS 3:2-3

Lord,

I thank You today for the evidence I see in my children that You are up to something grand in this family. Sometimes, Lord, I'm so encouraged when my children respond positively to my leading and teaching about You. Each one is "a letter from Christ" written in a human heart.

Remind my children through the day that their words and actions are being carefully "read" by others. May they be to others like a longed-for letter of encouragement from You, Lord.

O Spirit, write carefully in each of my children. Write amazing things, like when Your finger wrote the Ten Commandments on stone for Moses (Exod. 31:18). Let Your love for this world be written in my children's hearts so others—even future generations—may know You and praise You (Ps. 102:18).

Amen.

Prepared for His Presence

LORD, who may dwell in your sanctuary?

PSALM 15:1

PRAYING FROM PSALM 15

Dear Lord,

Today I claim with David the high goals for living that will prepare my children to enjoy Your presence and Your people:

—that my children will be blameless, that they will obey You and be known as the kids who really care about doing the right thing (v. 2);

—that my children's words will be truthful and caring and that they'll resist cutting remarks, sarcasm, or gossip. Help them to do good to others and think well of them (v. 3);

—that my children will avoid those who choose to be rude or obscene but will honor those who choose to revere You. Give them strength to keep their daily promises and their lifetime vows, even when keeping them is costly (v. 4);

—that my children will give to others generously, never with selfish motives and never accepting money to betray the truth or an innocent person (v. 5).

Then I know my children will be well-established in their lives and welcome in Your presence (vv. 1,5).

Amen.

Another Kind of Parent

*[Mordecai] had a beautiful and lovely young cousin, Hadassah (also
called Esther), whose father and mother were dead, and whom he had
adopted into his family and raised as his own daughter.*

ESTHER 2:7, TLB

Heavenly Father,

Today I pray about the other parent figures who will affect my child's
life for the better. I know that my loving arms won't always reach far
enough. How I thank You that You will use specially chosen relatives,
stepparents, teachers, and pastors to hug my children for me—to be
Your face and hands and voice in times of need.

Some of these people I may already know. Some I'll never meet.
Thank You, Lord, that You can call on other adults who love You to
carry out Your good purposes for each one of my children
(Isa. 49:22-23). Through her cousin Mordecai's pure motives and wise
advice, You took care of Esther, and You blessed Your people. Do the
same kind of miracles for my kids!

Bless these "other parents" who can encourage and love my kids in
ways I can't. When the call to parent comes, may they treasure my child
as much as You do. Also prepare me to be that "other parent" to children in my world.

But please, Lord, protect my kids from those adults who would
misuse or abuse their influence.

Heavenly Father, You have a special heart for children in need
(Ps. 146:9). How I thank You for Your amazing family on earth. I will
rest in Your wide, fatherly embrace today.

Amen.

"I Will Not Forget You!"

Can a mother forget the baby at her breast and have no compassion on the child she has borne? Though she may forget, I will not forget you! See, I have engraved you on the palms of my hands.

ISAIAH 49:15-16

Mighty God,

I am comforted by Your reassurances to the mothers and fathers of Israel when they cried out to You, "All that we treasured lies in ruins" (Isa. 64:11). Today I claim Your promised faithfulness and unending tenderness for my children for their whole lives:

    —I will contend with those who contend with you, and your children I will save (Isa. 49:25).

Thank You that You will fight for my children. If evil forces of any kind capture them, You will win them back. You have promised, mighty, loving God!

    —I will bring your children from the east and gather you from the west . . . everyone who is called by my name (Isa. 43:5,7).

Thank You that You will not let my children become lost from You. You will retrieve my sons and daughters from the ends of the earth, if necessary, because they are called by Your name and created for Your glory. You have promised, mighty, loving God!

    —I will pour out my Spirit on your offspring, and my blessing on your descendants (Isa. 44:3).

Thank You that You will give my children the full gift of Your Holy

Spirit. Your new life will spring up through them like poplar trees grow-ing beside a stream. You have promised, mighty, loving God!

My worship today is to trust You in these matters of the heart. You have never failed me. And You will not forget even one of Your promises to my children.

All praise in Jesus' dear name. Amen.

The Armor of God

The weapons we fight with are not the weapons of the world. On the contrary, they have divine power to demolish strongholds.

2 CORINTHIANS 10:4

PRAYING EPHESIANS 6:10-18

Lord,

Today I pray that You will equip my child for spiritual battles:

Help _____ to put on Your full armor so that when the day of evil comes, he may be able to stand his ground, and after he has done all he can do, to keep standing (v. 13).

Show my child how to buckle the belt of truth around her waist and how to fasten the breastplate of righteousness in place (v. 14).

Fit my child's feet with the readiness that comes from the gospel of peace (v. 15).

Give my child strength to take up the shield of faith, with which he can extinguish all the flaming arrows of the evil one (v. 16).

Assure my child, _____, that she wears the helmet of salvation, and help her take up the sword of the Spirit, which is Your Word (v. 17).

And after my child is clothed with Your armor, may he continue to stay alert to evil and pray at all times for himself and others (v. 18).

Amen.

When We Pray

he one concern of the devil is to keep the saints from prayer. He fears nothing from prayerless studies, prayerless work, prayerless religion. He laughs at our toil, mocks at our wisdom, but trembles when we pray.

JONATHAN EDWARDS

Building Blocks of Peace

No city or house divided against itself will stand.

MATTHEW 12:25, RSV

Lord of Peace,

You say it is good and pleasant when brothers (and sisters) live together in harmony (Ps. 133:1). You bless families where Your children get along (Ps. 133:3).

How I long for our family to be like the first Christians who were so changed by their new faith that they were one in heart and mind (Acts 4:32). O Lord, Prince of Peace, without Your help I don't think we can live like that!

And so today I ask You to help my children, especially _____ , choose peace. Help them lay down those ugly battle weapons—their own rights and preferences, their memories of little injustices, their comfortable old habits of nagging, teasing, or provoking each other. Show them instead how to pick up the building blocks of peace: pure motives, consideration, submission, fairness, mercy, and love (James 3:17).

Breathe into our home Your powerful Spirit of unity today so that with one clear voice our family may glorify You (Rom. 15:5) and show the world that You are real (John 17:23).

Amen.

Fools to the Bone

Some became fools through their rebellious ways and suffered affliction because of their iniquities.

PSALM 107:17

Lord,

I prove to myself on a daily basis how talented I am at being a fool in one way or another. Through silly pride and conceit, I try to live independently of You and Your strength. And unfortunately, I see that human tendency in my children as well.

But Your Word teaches that a fool is more than a person who behaves foolishly once in a while. These "fools to the bone" think they're so cool, so trendy, so much smarter than the ones who work hard and take responsibility. But these fools are headed for a hard life of disillusionment and suffering.

Spare my children, Lord, from becoming or being influenced by fools—movie screens and businesses and school hallways are packed with them. Especially today protect my kids from those who say—and act as if—there is no God (Ps. 14:1); those who are enslaved and deceived "by all kinds of passions and pleasures" (Titus 3:3); those who don't take the good advice of others (Prov. 12:15) and never seem to learn from their mistakes (Prov. 26:11).

By Your heavenly wisdom, show my children the disastrous consequences of a fool's life so they can see past the appeal of the moment.

And kindly forgive us of all our silly foolishnesses today.

Amen.

Above Every Name

He will be called Wonderful Counselor, Mighty God, Everlasting Father, Prince of Peace.

Dear Lord God,

Thank You that Your name is above every name:

You are our Wonderful Counselor. Your wisdom has been the foundation of all creation, yet it makes sense for my kids today. May my children hear Your voice in their inner ear: "This is the way. Walk in it." Thank You for taking pleasure in being this kind of God.

You are our Mighty God. We stand amazed before You today, our faces beaming with delight but with only limited comprehension, all because of one single reality: You are an awesome and powerful God! You are the only authority worthy of worship, and we do praise You.

You are our Everlasting Father. We are always Your children (Mom and Dad, too)—Your closest of kin! Until the end of time You will be my children's protector. You are always the one who knows and understands them best. Thank You that You always provide the affection, comfort, and fatherly encouragement they need the most.

You are our Prince of Peace. Your very presence brings peace to my children. Your power surrounds them with a mantle of blessing and contentment. How grateful I am that when my children feel at war with the whole world, You will take up their cause, helping them to overcome conflict and reconcile with others.

For all that Your names mean, I praise You and worship You, Lord. Our family testifies that You *do* live up to all Your names!

Amen.

Take Heart!

A happy heart makes the face cheerful, but heartache crushes the spirit.

PROVERBS 15:13

Heavenly Father,
Can I pour out my heart to You today? This parenting thing is a long
and exasperating process at times. Lately I've felt that so much of what
I'm doing is pointless; my kids aren't listening to me anyway, and no-
body around here notices all the work I do.

*I continually remember your work produced by faith, your labor
prompted by love, and your endurance inspired by hope in Me* (from
1 Thess. 1:3).

Thank You, Lord, for noticing and caring! Help me also to notice
when my kids choose to do the right thing—when they are kind to a
friend, share their prized possession, or actually help each other here at
home. I give You thanks for these glimpses of hope.

*Be joyful always; pray continually; give thanks in all circumstances, for
this is My will for you* (from 1 Thess. 5:16-18).

Yes, Lord, help me to keep praying, to joyfully expect the best of
my kids. Today in spite of frustrations—tattling, whining, or half-eaten
Pop-Tarts in the car—may I not grow weary in good parenting because
You've promised that all our efforts will bring results in due time
(Gal. 6:9).

Amen.

Lord, Teach Me to Care

ord, teach me to care, and not

to care. Teach me to sit still.

T S Eliot

The Great Healer

When Jesus had again crossed over by boat to the other side of the lake, . . . one of the synagogue rulers, named Jairus, came there. Seeing Jesus, he fell at his feet and pleaded earnestly with him, "My little daughter is dying. Please come and put your hands on her so that she will be healed and live." So Jesus went with him.

MARK 5:21-24

Dear Lord,
My child is really sick, and I'm worried about her. At these times I feel so helpless. Please come to our house today, as You did to Jairus's when You touched his little girl and made her well.

Thank You for caring so much about little miseries like swollen tonsils and measles and ear infections, as well as life-threatening afflictions. Thank You that You spent so much time healing people when You were on earth (Matt. 9:35). I know that You'll do the same for our family today.

You are the Great Physician. And You ask us simply to pray for healing. Lord, I believe You can heal with one touch, one word; exercise Your power even when my belief falls short (Mark 9:24). I will praise You even before I know the outcome (Jer. 17:14).

Bring others around me, including family members and church elders, who also believe that Your power is present today to heal (Luke 5:17, James 5:14-15). Give all of us the faith of Jairus, who came to You straightaway. Hear my plea. Heal my child, O Lord, and she shall be healed; rescue her, and she will be completely well (Jer. 17:14).

In Your powerful name. Amen.

Timeless Questions

You of little faith, why are you so afraid?

Jesus,

While You were here on earth, You talked freely with all kinds of people: worried fathers, young boys, sick little girls, desperate women, rich rulers, arrogant lawyers, frightened rabbis. And so many of these asked You questions. "Will You heal me?" or "How can this be . . . ?"

But sometimes You asked questions that echo down to me and my children even today. Help us to hear You, Lord, and to respond. How much more important are Your pointed and personal questions than any my kids will ever see on a test at school!

Do you believe that I am able to do this? (Matt. 9:28).

Lord, when those critical moments come in life—when my kids need healing or a job, or when they're praying for a friend in trouble—help them trust completely in Your power. Help them not only to believe that You can do anything but to go ahead and ask You (Matt. 21:22). For You are able to do more than anything they can imagine (Eph. 3:20).

What good will it be for a man if he gains the whole world, yet forfeits his soul? (Matt. 16:26).

Lord, as my kids pursue happiness—forming relationships, using their talents, pursuing success and financial stability—help them to see that nothing is as valuable in life as their souls. Convince them through experience that they would be fools to trade their spiritual well-being for any temporary pleasure or possession (1 Pet. 1:7).

What about you? . . . Who do you say I am? (Matt. 16:15).

Lord, I've had to answer this question repeatedly in my walk with You. Show my children, both through teaching and through their own personal encounters with You, that You are the Christ, the Son of God. And may this answer grow into a testimony to the whole world about who You are and what You can do (1 John 1:2-3).

And finally, Jesus, may my children continue to hear You asking them important questions all their lives:

"What will you do with the gifts I've given you?"

"Will you let go of the comfortable to reach for the significant?"

"Are you ready to forgive the one who has hurt you?"

"Do you love Me?"

"Do you really love Me?"

May their answers always bring You joy.

Amen.

"I Remember . . ."

Has [the Lord's] unfailing love vanished forever?

O God,

I pray for my children in those times when You seem to disappear without a trace. How much like babies we are, Lord—when we can't see You, we don't think You're here. And when my children can't see concrete evidence of Your love, they will so easily forget . . .

. . . what they learned in vacation Bible school or summer camp

. . . those cozy times in my lap, when they pointed over and over again to the same words and pictures or happily recited a favorite verse

. . . the good that came out of a tearful confession at our kitchen table

. . . the youth pastor's teaching

. . . the insights gleaned during a quiet moment with Your Word before they turned out the light.

At those risky times of forgetting, when doubt and disorientation could so easily trip my children up, please touch their memories. Bring to mind specific times when You've come through for them before. Remind them of those times when, like the Israelites, they lost sight of You but "your path led through the sea, . . . though your footprints were not seen" (Ps. 77:19).

May they declare with Asaph, "I remembered You, O God. . . . I will remember your miracles" (Ps. 77:3,11).

Amen.

A Family at Shiloh

Go now to the place in Shiloh where I first made a dwelling for my Name, and . . . I spoke to you again and again.

JEREMIAH 7:12-13

O Lord who dwells among us,
I bow in Your presence in this moment of quietness to tell You that You are the ruler, owner, source, and explanation for my life! And not just mine. I speak on behalf of my whole family today. My children and I honor and exalt You. May we live out this worshipful attitude in all our actions today.

We want Your holy presence to shine in our home, to be obvious to every adult and child who comes through the door. May Your name somehow receive glory today amid all the pandemonium of our noisy household.

Yes, King and Lord of this house, reign here today. May my children give You control over all that is said and done. May their thoughts and intentions, the way they treat each other, and how we all treat You swirl together like incense rising in the temple courtyard. Rising up to You . . .

May the fragrance of our worship rise in the morning sun as it did at Shiloh during the days of Samuel as families gathered and watched and prayed and made their vows and presented their simple offerings to You—and were so happy to be called "God's chosen people."

"The LORD continued to appear at Shiloh, and there he revealed himself to Samuel through his word" (1 Sam. 3:21).

Thank You, Lord. Amen.

To Respect and Honor

Children, the right thing for you to do is to obey your parents as those whom the Lord has set over you. The first commandment to contain a promise was: Honour thy father and thy mother that it may be well with thee, and that thou mayest live long on the earth.

EPHESIANS 6:1-3, PH

Heavenly Father,

Thank You for the honor of being a parent. Help me to carry out my role so that my children's potential is realized and so they can honor their parents as You ask them to.

I pray today for a home environment of respect where my children practice good manners, consideration, deference, and patience. You have put us, along with teachers and other leaders, in authority for a reason (Rom. 13:1). And You ask children to obey for a reason—so their lives will go better. Even the Lord Jesus lived under Your authority while on earth, saying that pleasing You and finishing the work You asked Him to do was like food to Him (John 4:34).

With a firm and loving hand, may I encourage cheerful obedience from each of my children today. Especially help my kids when they have an unpopular or unlikable teacher; may they see past the person and choose obedience because of Your command.

As they make a habit of respecting those in authority, I thank You that You'll bless them in school and work, in marriage, and in their civic responsibilities (Luke 19:17). When they look back on their lives, may they be able to declare with David, "This has been my practice: I obey Your precepts" (Ps. 119:56).

Amen.

Whole All Through

Surely you desire truth in the inner parts; you teach me wisdom in the inmost place.

PSALM 51:6

Dear Lord,

I spend all day trying to shape my children's characters, but I can only work from the outside. I'm afraid I may not be getting through. Lord, You hardly look at the outside because You know that the inside is what matters (1 Sam. 16:7). How can I teach my children integrity?

I worry sometimes that my kids will grow up having mastered all the right words and actions but not be changed through and through by You. Then they'll fold when the pressure mounts.

Lord, use Your Spirit and Your Word to penetrate their innermost natures (Heb. 4:12). Make them whole and healed all through so that the beauty people see on the outside is true of their hearts as well. Only You can accomplish this, Lord.

Help me to model integrity. Help me demonstrate that what I appear to be in public is who I am in private. May my kids see me taking all the advice I give.

Save my children and me from deceiving ourselves—and along the way keep making us whole all through by Your work of grace (Ps. 119:29).

Amen.

Caught in the Act

You may be sure that your sin will find you out.

Heavenly Father,

How well I know the shame of getting caught in sin and the pain of the discipline that follows. Yet, "the punishment you gave me was the best thing that could have happened to me, for it taught me to pay attention to your laws. They are more valuable to me than millions in silver and gold!" (Ps. 119:71-72, TLB).

Today I pray that my children would be caught quickly when they've done wrong, especially if they're hiding what they've done or are persisting in it. Your Word says we can become tied up and helpless in our own sins (Prov. 5:22). Spare my kids, loving Father, from the serious consequences of unaddressed sin. Don't let them be among those whose misdeeds dog them for years just under the surface (1 Tim. 5:24).

So catch my kids, Lord! And if I'm the one who uncovers the problem, help me to restore my child gently, keeping in mind my own enormous vulnerabilities (Gal. 6:1).

You know my heart, Lord. This isn't a mean prayer but one that's full of hope and reverence. Why? Because Your nature, holy as it is, is also adorned by goodness, mercy, and a longing to forgive (Ps. 130:3-4).

In Your gracious name. Amen.

Praying Beyond Words

*The Spirit also helps us in our present limitations. For example, we do
not know how to pray worthily, but his Spirit within us is actually
praying for us in those agonising longings which cannot find words. He
who knows the heart's secrets understands the Spirit's intentions as he
prays . . . for those who love [God].*

ROMANS 8:26-27, PH

Holy Spirit,

Help me to pray for my children. Talk through me; talk in spite of me.
You said I was made for this holy conversation, but I have so many
limitations.

My prayers for my children are hindered by impure motives, poor
discernment, and long lapses.

Forgive these unworthy prayers, Holy Lord. I do want to pray well
for my children. Thank You that Your Word helps to focus my thoughts
and desires, revealing to me "the mind of Christ" in so many family
matters.

But today I simply say, "Come, Holy Spirit. Pray for me beyond
words." You know my concerns about my children; You are one with
God's good purposes. I trust You utterly!

How I love You, God! You are near me now, listening even when I
stammer and stop. You are not a far-off God, waiting for me to say just
the right thing before You act (Acts 17:27-28, Ps. 145:18).

Today, Lord, it is good to pray beyond words. You are in Your holy
temple—it is *good* to keep silent before You and wait in quietness and
confidence for You to answer (Hab. 2:20, Isa. 30:15).

Amen.

A Better Way

Love must be sincere. Hate what is evil; cling to what is good.

ROMANS 12:9

PRAYING FROM PROVERBS 6

Lord,

Today I pray that You will help my children to hate what You hate.
Your Word lists seven things that are detestable to You (6:16-19). Please
keep these choices, attitudes, and actions from my children's lives today.
For each of these, show us a better way:

—*Haughty eyes.* May my children be motivated by compassion and
wisdom, not by self-centeredness and pride. You are the meek Savior;
help my kids to long to be like You. Show me how to deal lovingly and
insightfully with "I'm better than you" attitudes.

—*A lying tongue.* Lord, help me nurture in my children a passion
for truth—honesty and integrity that begin in the heart and express
themselves in every relationship. Help them to be aware of and reject
convenient exaggerations and "white lies."

—*Hands that shed innocent blood.* Graft into my children's natures a
distaste for taking advantage of easy victims—a younger sibling, an unpopular or disadvantaged playmate. Instead, may my children be defenders of the weak, and may their hands and consciences be clean.

—*A heart that devises wicked schemes.* Whether with their friends at
the mall or alone on the Internet, my kids need Your help to resist plans
and activities that are obviously wrong or dangerous. At key moments
give them the boldness to say, "No, that's not a smart idea."

—*Feet that are quick to rush into evil.* How often, Lord, my kids just react without thinking. By Your Spirit and my example, help them to stop and think. Help them to see past the excitement of the moment to the probable consequences and reject what's wrong.

—*A false witness who pours out lies.* Keep my children from slander, gossip, and other ways of hurting others' feelings or reputations through what they say. May they choose only true and encouraging words.

—*A man who stirs up dissension among brothers.* Lord, You have called my children to be peacemakers. May they develop a holy hatred for conflict in the family in all its forms—teasing, quarreling, accusing, tattling, and playing one person against another.

Continue Your beautiful work of sanctification in my children today. May I be Your agent of love, showing a better way and nudging my children toward pleasing You. Thank You for Your Holy Spirit who helps us and blesses us with peace and grace.

Amen.

Courage to Reach for the Best

For God did not give us a spirit of timidity, but a spirit of power, of love and of self-discipline. . . . I pray that you . . . may be filled to the measure of all the fullness of God.

2 TIMOTHY 1 7; EPHESIANS 3:17,19

Lord Jesus,

It is my joy and honor to pray for my children. Each one is a miracle in the making, growing from year to year into a creation that only You can see completely (Ps. 139:16). I absolutely believe in this miracle going on right under my nose!

Yes, O God of miracles, I know it's happening—in spite of ill, cranky, foolish, wandering, and obstinate kids (and their parents). I know it's happening in spite of my inability to see the miracle or on some days even to care much about it. Yes, You are up to something grand here! Lord, today I ask that You would grow in my children the courage to want, reach for, and cherish Your best. We do not want to be like those who give up on our destiny and are lost (Heb. 10:39, PH). You changed cowardly, small-spirited fishermen into world ambassadors, leaders, and heroes of faith. Change us too, Lord! You are able to do immeasurably more than all we ask or imagine, because Your immense power is at work in us (Eph. 3:20).

Fearfulness and timidity are *never* what You give! Instead, Your gifts to us through Your Spirit are

—power to overcome all obstacles,

—love that changes us and those we love,

—self-discipline to stay the course (2 Tim. 1:7).

You, Lord, are the strength of our lives (Ps 27:1). Thank You that any success my children realize in reaching for their futures will not have to be accomplished only by their limited strength or resolution but will be granted by Your Spirit (Zech. 4:6).

I pray especially for _____ today. May she be a willing accomplice, a co-conspirator, and a wholehearted candidate for Your best today.

I praise You, Lord Jesus, that You remain faithful when we don't (2 Tim. 2:13). I claim Your mighty power and Your unfailing promises on behalf of my child.

Jesus of miracles, let me tell You something from this house today: We believe in You, and we love You!

Amen.

"I'm First"

An argument started among the disciples as to which of them would be the greatest.

LUKE 9:46

Lord,

I know that sound of voices squabbling about who comes first. Oh, do I! First in, first out, first to open, first to take a turn, first to ride, first up front, first for seconds.

"I'm first . . ." is such an instinctive reflex, Lord. But You want to show my children a better way: "If anyone wants to be first, he must be the very last, and the servant of all" (Mark 9:35).

Teach my children, Lord, to be first to offer, first to step back, first to share, first to speak up for the quiet one, first to serve, first to say, "You first."

Lord, when You taught Your disciples about who's first in Your kingdom, You took a little child, put Your arms around him, and looked in his face. Then You said, "Whoever humbles himself like this child is the greatest in the kingdom of heaven" (Matt. 18:4).

This is my plea: When You come to our house today, may You find my children second in line—with the first place saved for You.

Amen.

The Meeting Place

For the Word that God speaks is alive and active; it cuts more keenly
than any two-edged sword: it strikes through to the place where soul and
spirit meet, to the innermost intimacies of a man's being: it examines the
very thoughts and motives of a man's heart.

HEBREWS 4:12, PH

Lord,

How I long to be with You in that meeting place of soul and spirit and
for each of my children to find You there. May they follow Your words
to find You, like Hansel and Gretel followed crumbs to find their way
back home.

Every day may my children reach for their Bibles. And no matter
their age, may their reading lead to a personal encounter with You without which the day just wouldn't be the same.

Help them to get through all the unfamiliar Maher-Shalal-Hash-
Baz names (Isa. 8:3) and the difficult "circumcision of the heart" con-
cepts (Rom. 2:29). By Your Spirit, "alive and active," compensate for
any limitations of their reading and thinking skills. Take them right to
that meeting place of Spirit with spirit. Open their minds, as You did
for the disciples so they can understand and respond to the Scriptures
(Luke 24:25).

Teach them to wait—through confusing questions, through miss-
ing information, through doubts, through silence.

Thank You, Lord, that when my children meet with You regularly
and act on Your life-giving words—not forgetting what they've heard—
they will be blessed in everything they do (James 1:25).

Amen.

A Scientist in Ecstasy

I thank Thee, my Creator and Lord, that Thou hast given me these joys in Thy creation, this ecstasy over the works of Thy hands. I have made known the glory of Thy works to men as far as my finite spirit was able to comprehend Thy infinity. If I have said anything wholly unworthy of Thee, or have aspired after my own glory, graciously forgive me. Amen.

JOHANN KEPLER

A Creation Celebration

We are God's workmanship, created in Christ Jesus to do good works,
which God prepared in advance for us to do.

EPHESIANS 2:10

Dear Heavenly Father,

My child, _____, is Your special creation, anticipated by You
from before the beginning of time, now reborn in Jesus to carry out
Your perfect will (Eph. 2:10).

You are the Great Creator God (Gen. 1:1). Everything You imagine
and shape is good (1 Tim. 4:4). How grateful I am that Your unchang-
ing goodness will surround my child throughout this life (Ps. 23:6).
And when Your personal, loving intentions for my child are realized,
You will exclaim, "It is good!" Like the tiniest flower on Creation Day,
my child is the skilled, caring work of Your fingers. How excellent is
Your name in all the earth (Ps. 8:1)!

That's why I can be confident that what You have started in my
child's life You will certainly finish (Phil. 1:6). Regardless of life's
troubles, I can rest assured that because of Your loving work in my
child, he will shine like the brightness of the stars forever and ever
(Dan. 12:3).

Until that celebration day, breathe into my child the will and the
power to seek You, to be molded by Your hands, to honor You with a
life of goodness (Phil. 2:13).

Amen.

A Blessing for Patience

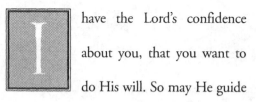 have the Lord's confidence about you, that you want to do His will. So may He guide you into an ever deeper understanding of the love of God and the patience of Christ.

FROM 2 THLSSALONIANS 3:4-5

Love Is Patient

Love is patient, love is kind.

1 CORINTHIANS 13:4

Dear Lord,

Your patience was tested so often when You tried to teach Your disciples the ways of the kingdom. You put up with heat and dirt, hunger and complaining, foolishness and stubbornness, irresponsibility and laziness. But You proved Yourself a patient and compassionate teacher. You are slow to anger, abounding in love (Ps. 103:8).

How can I be more like You? I'm slow to love and quick to lose my temper. Forgive me, Lord, and help me today. Please give me Your amazing peace and strength—then I'll do better at enduring the complaining, disobedience, and foot-dragging that often does me in.

I don't want my impatient response to stand in my child's way or discredit my faith. Help me instead to be Your servant in my family by keeping my head cool and my heart at peace (2 Cor. 6:3-6).

When my kids are just being kids, may I bear with them in love (Eph. 4:2). When they oppose me, help me to instruct them gently, confident that over time You will help them see things clearly, escape Satan's traps, and arrive at a lifelong grasp of the truth (2 Tim. 2:25-26).

Lord, Your Word says that my impatience is often caused ultimately by my pride (Eccles. 7:8). Show me if this is so. I give You permission to test my nerves today, because I know Your goal is my honest desire—to make me more like You (James 1:4; Rom. 5:3-5).

Amen.

Miracles Happen Here

He did miracles in the sight of their fathers.

PSALM 78:12

O Lord,

You are "the God who performs miracles" (Psalm 77:14). Thank You that my children can *expect* miracles in their lives because the extraordinary and impossible are easy for You. All Your works are marvels, those in us and those around us (Psalm 147). You made the whole universe by Your amazing power (Acts 14:15), and then You broke through the laws of Your awesome universe to bring us salvation through Jesus Christ (Heb. 2:3-4).

Thank You that with the same incomparably great power that raised Jesus from the dead, You are at work right now in my children (Eph. 1:18-20). Truly, nothing is too hard for You (Jer. 32:17)!

Help my children to remember their mighty heavenly Father in every difficult choice or struggle. Thank You that You are making us like Jesus—that when we see Him, we *will* be completely changed by His beauty (1 John 3:2). What an awesome miracle that will be!

Make this a day of miracles. Nothing less will do. Yes, Lord, do Your miracles in the sight of Mom and Dad today, and in the lives of each child in our house.

Thank You that something good can happen at any moment—because we love You. And help us not to miss it when it does!

I ask with faith and gratitude in Jesus' name. Amen.

Little Insights

You discern my going out and my lying down; you are familiar with all my ways.

PSALM 139:3

PRAYING FROM PSALM 139

Lord,
You have searched my child's innermost being and know her intimately (v. 1). I'm so glad! As a parent, I often feel I am just scratching the surface of her life. I only see what she lets me see. Yet there is so much more to her that only You know (v. 3).

What *is* she thinking, Lord? Sometimes when she tries to tell me something, I'm impatient with her unrevealing description of her day or her feelings.

But You know her heart before a word is on her tongue (v. 4). You know what she is thinking, even if her vocabulary is limited to "yeah," "cool," "fine," and "Where's the phone?"

Today, Jesus, lover of my child, would You reveal a little bit more of her to me? Give me Your insight to understand important mysteries of her personality right now. I want to see past the tears or smiles to who she really is.

May I never use what she's told me about herself to hurt or manipulate her in any way. I only want to communicate better, give better advice, and love her in the way she needs today.

Thank You for the marvelous idea You had when You thought of my child and planned her life (vv. 15-16)!

Amen.

Into All the World

Go into all the world and preach the good news to all creation.

MARK 16:15

Heavenly Father,

What a privilege it is to be able to pray for my children to be witnesses in the world for You!

You promised that if my children confessed Jesus as Lord with their mouths and believed You raised Him from the dead for them, they would be saved (Rom. 10:9). My prayer today is that my kids will grow up feeling so motivated by this truth that no one will need to prod them to share the good news of salvation.

In fact, Lord, may they be so genuinely overwhelmed by Your love that they wouldn't think of *not* telling their friends, neighbors, and even strangers about You (2 Tim. 1:7-8). May they be willing to spread the message even to the ends of the earth (Mark 16:15).

As my children are growing up and struggling with insecurities, blemishes, and changing bodies, help them to be bold about the one thing they can feel confident about—Jesus is the only way (John 14:6)!

Remind them that they can overcome any obstacle Satan throws in their path by proclaiming what You've done for them (Rev. 12:11).

May my children say with Paul many times throughout their lives, "I am not ashamed of the gospel, because it is the power of God for the salvation of everyone who believes" (Rom. 1:16).

Amen.

Speaking Well of Others

But if anyone does sin, we have one who speaks to the Father in our defense—Jesus Christ, the Righteous One.

1 JOHN 2:1

Savior and Lord,

Thank You that You speak well of me and my children to the Father! I have confidence, knowing that You are always interceding for us (Rom. 8:34; Heb. 7:25). And when Satan comes to speak against us day and night (Rev. 12:10), You are there to defend us.

Today I pray that my children will learn how to talk kindly about other people (Titus 3:1-2). Help them to resist repeating negative things because it makes them feel powerful to know something others don't— "Did you know that Meagan got caught smoking?"

Show my children that it is not only wrong to rejoice in others' mistakes, but it's wrong even to listen to such talk. Your Word says that without an audience, a gossiper gives up, and a rumor has a chance to die down (Prov. 26:20).

Help my kids learn that though gossip may seem harmless, the words go deep into our spirits and affect us as we say or hear them (Prov. 18:8). Help us instead to be more like Christ—defenders, not accusers, of others.

Amen.

A Blessing for Overcoming Temptation

I bless you, _____, in Jesus' name to overcome temptation today. May you experience firsthand God's trustworthiness and care in your time of testing. May you see the way of escape and take it—and celebrate your deliverance with us soon!

FROM 1 CORINTHIANS 10:13

Escaping Temptation

No temptation has seized you except what is common to man. And God is faithful; he will not let you be tempted beyond what you can bear. But when you are tempted, he will also provide a way out so that you can stand up under it.

1 CORINTHIANS 10:13

Heavenly Father,

My child is facing temptation. He is up against forces stronger than he is—and he doesn't even know it! His desires pull him away from You. The world, with all its enticements, sucks him down. And Satan roars like a lion (1 John 2:16, 1 Pet. 5:8)—but my child doesn't hear!

O Father, save him! Don't let evil wound or trap him. Make a way of escape today, as You've promised (Ps. 18:35, 1 Cor. 10:13). Lead my child away from temptations (Matt. 6:13); let him see those "opportunities" for what they really are—dead ends (James 1:15).

By Your power, block evil people from influencing his desires and his actions (Ps. 140:1).

Turn his eyes away from worthless things; renew his commitments to Your truth (Ps. 119:37). Bring Your Word, hidden in his memory, into his thoughts; use it to keep him from sin (Ps. 119:11).

Thank You that You are a faithful Savior who rescues Your own (2 Pet. 2:9). All attractions but You fade away (Ps. 102:12). Show my child today that the person who follows You has the best life (1 John 2:17)!

Amen.

An Evening Prayer

ay there fall upon me now, O God, a great sense of Thy power and Thy Glory, so that I may see all earthly things in their true measure.

Let me not be ignorant of this great thing, that one day is with Thee as a thousand years and a thousand years as one day.

Give me now such understanding of Thy perfect holiness as will make an end of all pride in my own attainment.

Grant unto me now such a vision of Thine uncreated beauty as will make me dissatisfied with all lesser beauties.

JOHN BAILLIE

Fears in the Night

For I am the LORD, your God, who takes hold of your right hand and says to you, Do not fear; I will help you.

ISAIAH 41:13

Heavenly Father,

Sometimes my child is tormented by fears at night. Today I pray that he will learn more about the God who always holds on tightly to his hand (Isa. 41:13).

Long after my child and I have checked under the bed and prayed together, may he hear You saying, "I will never leave you helpless. I'll never let you down. I'll never let go of you" (from Heb. 13:5).

Thank You, Father, that You never want my child to suffer from needless fears—You've given him Your own Spirit of power, love, and self-discipline (2 Tim. 1:7). Instead of being a slave to fearfulness, he can be free in the knowledge that he belongs to You. At any time, day or night, he can call out, "Abba, Father," and You will be there for him (Rom. 8:15).

Tonight may my child hear Your voice saying, "Don't be afraid" (John 14:27). By Your Spirit and by my faithful example, I look forward to the time when he will learn to say with joy and confidence, "The Lord is my helper; I will not be afraid!" (Heb. 13:6).

Amen.

Hidden Words

I have hidden your word in my heart that I might not sin against you.

Dear Lord,

I long for my children to grow up loving the Bible. I know they're young in the faith now, but I want them to learn early to crave the spiritual food of Scripture so they can grow strong in their faith (1 Pet. 2:2, Rom. 10:17). My hope for them is that they will be like the Bereans who "received the message with great eagerness and examined the Scriptures every day" (Acts 17:11).

May our home be a place where the Bible is respected, talked about—and used! May we treasure Your Word, Lord. May my kids learn to use it like a powerful sword against evil (Eph. 6:17) and as an answer book for their big questions (Prov. 22:21).

Show me how to be a good example and a wise problem solver as I nurture my children into Bible-reading habits that will last a lifetime. In the days ahead bring each truth or verse hidden in their memories to life at the right moment, influencing their desires, words, and thoughts.

Today, Lord, may Your words of life that are securely held and treasured in their hearts keep my children from sin (Ps. 119:9). And may they experience an exhilarating freedom of spirit today—because they have filled up on Your Word (Ps. 119:45).

Amen.

A Passion for Purity

Flee from sexual immorality. All other sins a man commits are outside his body, but he who sins sexually sins against his own body. Do you not know that your body is a temple of the Holy Spirit, who is in you, whom you have received from God? You are not your own; you were bought at a price. Therefore honor God with your body.

1 CORINTHIANS 6:18-20

Lord,

I pray that my children will develop a passion for purity that is even greater than the urgency of the sexual drive You have given them. May they always think of their bodies as Your dwelling place and want to keep them pure for You (1 Cor. 6:19). Help my kids to feel they can bring their questions about sex to me. Please give me the right words in awkward moments so I can help them feel at ease, as well as answer them clearly, fully, and with confidence (Prov. 25:11). Nudge me when it's the right time to pass on an important attitude or piece of information, even if my kids aren't asking for it.

O Lord, these are such tough times for a teenager who wants to be pure. Please, Lord, give my children strength to hold on to what they've been taught about these things from a young age (Prov. 3:1).

I pray that my children will see through the barrage of false and immoral messages about sexuality portrayed on TV and in movies. Fill my children with a genuine and enthusiastic desire to save sex for marriage.

Lord, please use every important influence in Your power—spiritual conviction, our example, their Christian friends' belief systems, medical facts, and even their own logic—to add up to a winning case for the wisdom and value of abstinence until marriage. Keep Satan from succeeding in making my kids think it's futile to try to be sexually pure or that because they are tempted, they are evil and might as well give in. Remind them that You were tempted, Lord. But because You remained sinless, You have power and compassion to help when they are tempted (Heb. 2:18).

Show my children that it is actually courageous to run away at the first sign of sexual temptation (2 Tim. 2:22). Help them to avoid situations where they could fall prey to lust (James 1:14). Signal them when it's time to say, "Please don't do that," or "I think I'd better take you home."

Above all, Lord, may abstinence not seem to them a sacrifice as much as a way to guard a wonderful treasure. May my children grow up knowing that sex is a gift from You worth celebrating and protecting.

Amen.

The Heart's Treasure

We are looking all the time not at the visible things but at the invisible.
The visible things are transitory: it is the invisible things that are really
permanent.

2 CORINTHIANS 4:18, PH

Lord,

Today I pray that You will teach my children to choose goals and objectives in life that have eternal value. Help me to teach them from a young age to recognize the difference between an earthly and a heavenly treasure: Can it break, rust, or outwear its warranty? Is it collectible (Matt. 6:19-21)? Or is it something unseen that will last forever—like salvation, grace, peace, and joy (2 Cor. 4:18)?

Lord, it seems that everywhere my kids turn they're bombarded by slick sales pitches and pressured by their peers to be consumers and pleasure seekers. It's not having clothes they worry about; it's having the right clothes! It's not needs that drive them—and me—but endless wants.

May my children decide not to serve what money or fame can buy but choose instead to serve *You* (Matt. 6:24). I know it is possible for our family to live in such a way that it is obvious to all that our real treasure is incorruptible (1 Pet. 1:3-6).

Fill our family with wisdom, Lord. Show us how to seek You first. Then we'll have the true treasures of the heart that You promise (Matt. 6:33).

Amen.

A Good Friend

A friend loves at all times.

PROVERBS 17:17

Lord,

You are my friend, and You call me friend (John 15:14). I know that friendship is important to You.

I pray that my children will have many friends and that their friends will love You and do what it is right (Prov. 13:20). Bring my children friends who are as loyal as brothers or sisters might be (Prov. 18:24). Guide my children to choose friends who will help them get back on their feet when they fail (Eccles. 4:10).

Show my children how to develop friendships that will last a long time, friends who will love them at all times (Prov. 17:17)—when it is easy and fun and when it is hard, painful, or tiring.

Above all, I pray that my children will learn from You how to be a true friend. Show them how to lay down their lives—how to make important sacrifices—for friends (John 15:13).

Finally, I pray that my child will love You so much that he will be called a friend of God (James 2:23).

Amen.

Gifts of Grace

May my meditation be pleasing to him, as I rejoice in the LORD.

PSALM 104:34

MEDITATIONS TO CARRY THROUGH THE DAY

Lord, You are able to make all grace
abound to my child, _____,
so that in all things at all times,
having all that he or she needs,
my child will abound in every good work.
(2 Cor. 9:8)

Having been justified by Your grace,
_____ has become an heir,
having the hope of eternal life.
(Titus 3:7)

Your grace is sufficient for _____,
for Your power is made perfect in weakness.
(2 Cor. 12:9)

A Blessing for a New Venture

ay the LORD answer you when you are in distress; may the name of the God of Jacob protect you. May he send you help from the sanctuary. . . . May he give you the desire of your heart and make all your plans succeed.

PSALM 20:1-2,4

21:21

He who pursues righteousness and love finds life, prosperity and honor.

PROVERBS 21:21

Heavenly Father,

As my child, _____, approaches twenty-one and steps out to pursue his dreams, thank You that *every single* promise You have given me in prayer for his life will hold true in his journey ahead (1 Pet. 1:25). I love You, Lord, for being that kind of Father to my children.

Today my petition is that You will bring to _____'s mind Your "21:21" rule from Proverbs. May he, as Solomon advised, write it permanently on the tablet of his heart (Prov. 7:3).

May he *pursue righteousness.* May he be careful to lead a blameless life before You, walking in his house and among his friends with a clean heart (Ps. 101:2), striving to please You in every decision.

May he *pursue love.* May he love You first as his Lord and God, putting You before every other affection or activity—and may he faithfully express Your sacrificial love to others (Matt. 22:37-38).

Help me to continue to be an example in these priorities, for Your glory and my child's continual encouragement.

Then I know, Heavenly Father, that You will bring him the kind of *life, prosperity, and honor* You've had in mind for him since time began. And all our thanks and praise will be for You alone! Amen.

With a Loud Trumpet

For the Lord himself will come down from heaven, with a loud command, with the voice of the archangel and with the trumpet call of God, and the dead in Christ will rise first. After that, we who are still alive and are left will be caught up together with them in the clouds to meet the Lord in the air. And so we will be with the Lord forever. Therefore encourage each other with these words.

1 THESSALONIANS 4:16-18

Lord of the Universe,
You are coming back!

How often I forget to rejoice in this fact, to watch the sky, to remind my kids about it, to even consider that today might be the day. Today may our whole family be encouraged as we listen to Your promises:

Behold, I am coming soon! My reward is with me, and I will give to everyone according to what he has done. I am the Alpha and the Omega, the First and the Last, the Beginning and the End (Rev. 22:12-13).

How we praise You, Lord of the Universe, Coming One, Alpha and Omega, Beginning and End! In the middle of a muddled week, may my children and I recall who You really are! It's so amazing to me that You care about our little family.

You will be My people, and I Myself will be with you and be your God. I will wipe every tear from your eyes. There will be no more death or mourning or crying or pain. I will make everything new! (from Rev. 21:3-5).

Thank You for Your words of comfort, Lord. Thank You for

promising to make everything new, including Mom, Dad and all the kids. It's so good to know that we will not always be stuck in these owie- and illness-prone bodies of ours.

At the last trumpet, you will all be changed—in a flash, in the twinkling of an eye. The dead will be raised imperishable, and you will be changed (from 1 Cor. 15:51-52).

Thank You most of all that someday my children and I *will* finally see You, Lord. And when we see You as You really are, all that You've been working on in us during these ordinary days will finally be complete (1 John 3:2).

At that time you will see Me coming in a cloud with power and great glory. When these things begin to take place, stand up and lift up your heads, because your redemption is drawing near (from Luke 21:27).

Yes, Lord, we will lift up our heads! Because we have this hope, today my kids and I will seek You with all our hearts (1 John 3:3). We will dream of You, talk to one another about Your return, and listen for the sound of trumpets.

Amen.

NOTES

An Invitation

1. David M. Dawson, *More Power in Prayer* (Grand Rapids: Zondervan, 1942), 104.

2. Francois Fénelon, as quoted in *A Guide to Prayer*, ed. Reuben P. Job and Morman Shawchuck (Nashville: Upper Room Books, 1983), 56.

Chapter 1

1. Karl Barth, cited "In God's Kingdom . . . Prayer Is Social Action," John Robb with Larry Wilson, *World Vision*, vol. 41, no. 1, February/March 1997, 5.

2. Unpublished letters to the editor, *Christian Parenting Today*, September 1992.

Chapter 2

1. Charles Mortimer Guilbert, *The Book of Common Prayer* (Kingsport, Tenn.: Kingsport Press, 1977), 336.

2. C. S. Lewis, *The Joyful Christian*, quoted in Bob Benson Sr. and Michael W. Benson, *Disciplines of the Inner Life* (Nashville: Generoux/Nelson, 1989), 272.

3. Wayne R. Spear, *The Theology of Prayer* (Grand Rapids: Baker, 1979), 59.

4. Spear, *The Theology of Prayer*, 57.

5. Henri J. M. Nouwen, *With Open Hands* (New York: Ballantine Books/Epiphany, 1985), 3-8.

6. Richard J. Foster, *Prayers from the Heart* (San Francisco: HarperSanFrancisco, 1994), xiv.

Quotations

John Baillie, quoted in Bruce Shelley, *All the Saints Adore Thee* (Grand Rapids: Zondervan, 1988), 206.

Joe Bayly, *Psalms of My Life* (Colorado Springs, Colo.: Lifejourney Books, 1987).

Carlo Carretto, "The Way of Freedom," from *Selected Writings*, ed. Robert Ellsberg (Maryknoll, N. Y.: Orbis Books, 1994), 74-75.

Richard Foster, *Prayer* (San Francisco: HarperSanFrancisco, 1992), 196.

Johann Kepler, quoted in *A Treasury of Great Prayers*, ed. Donald T. Kauffman (Westwood, N. J.: Revell, 1964), 27.

Brother Lawrence, quoted in *The Book of Joy*, trans. Sherwood Wirt (New York: McCracken Press, 1994).

George Macdonald, quoted in *The Lord of the Journey*, ed. Roger Pooley and Philip Seddon (San Francisco: Collins Liturgical, 1987), 227.

Andrew Murray, *The Ministry of Intercession*, from *The Andrew Murray Collection* (Uhrichsville, Ohio: Barbour, 1954).

Andrew Murray, *The Prayer Life* (London: Morgan and Scott, 1914), 100.

Warren Myers with Ruth Myers, *Pray: How to Be Effective in Prayer* (Singapore: Navigators, 1982).

Karl Rahner, *Prayers for a Lifetime*, ed. Albert Raffelt (New York: Crossroad, 1995), 23.

Bruce Shelley, *All the Saints Adore Thee* (Grand Rapids: Zondervan, 1988), 205.

John Wesley, quoted in *A Treasury of Great Prayers*, ed. Donald T. Kauffman (Westwood, N. J.: Revell, 1964), 19.

Title Index

Topical Index

Printed in the United States
by Baker & Taylor Publisher Services